Toy Train Repair Made Easy

21 LIONEL POSTWAR PROJECTS

Ray L. Plummer

KALMBACH
BOOKS

Printed in the United States of America

99 00 01 02 03 04 05 06 07 08   10 9 8 7 6 5 4 3 2 1

Visit our website at
http://books.kalmbach.com
Secure online ordering available

Publisher's Cataloging in Publication
(Provided by Quality Books, Inc.)

Plummer, Ray L.
    Toy train repair made easy : 21 Lionel postwar
projects / Ray L. Plummer. — 1st ed.
    p. cm.
    ISBN: 0-89778-508-8

    1. Railroads—Models—Maintenance and repair.
2. Lionel Corporation. I. Title. II. Title:
Repairing Lionel trains

TF197.P5 1999   625.1'9'0288
                           QBI99-673

Book and cover design: Kristi Ludwig

Contents

—

Introduction

This is a book for people who love to *operate* Lionel toy trains and would like to learn how to *repair* them as well.

I've often said that the first train collector was probably a guy whose locomotive quit running, so he put it on the mantelpiece. When his friends asked him about it, he was too embarrassed to admit that it didn't work anymore and he didn't know how to fix it, so he told them that he was starting a collection.

Because there were a lot of trains in that condition out there, the idea caught on. To this day, the "collector types" will tell you they don't care whether the train runs or not, as long as it looks good on the shelf.

I think most of those guys are blowing smoke without a pellet. Electric trains were made to *run*, and most of them will do so indefinitely with regular lubrication, minor tune-ups, and occasional heavier repairs.

It's amazing to most people accustomed to our "throwaway" society, where the planned obsolescence goes in before the name goes on, just how well these old Lionel "toys" were put together. They were designed to be taken apart and repaired easily, as any young train owner with a screwdriver could testify.

Lionel trains and accessories traditionally employed rather simple technology, most of which could be understood, if not mastered, by the children who played with them. Uncomplicated low-voltage electrical circuits, powered by transformers with safety devices built into them, ran everything the company made. Young train owners were encouraged to experiment. Trains and train-related paraphernalia found their way into many a school project, and not just in shop class.

Electric trains taught basic laws of mechanics and physics to boys who were unaware they were being "educated" in the process. Those who built layouts also learned carpentry, design, and more artistic things. If the layout had more than one train, it taught planning and organization as well as logistics and timing. Operating the trains sharpened motor skills and coordination. Social and political considerations in acquiring space and allowing other family members to participate were quickly learned.

The focus of this book is on helping you keep your trains running and accessories working as they were intended.

Basic care and maintenance required to keep the trains in good condition and running smoothly not only taught responsibility, it sparked intellectual curiosity and encouraged logical problem-solving when the operations broke down. Those of us with enabling parents conducted our own inquiries into the mechanics of our trains. We knew *how* they worked long before we understood *why*.

We knew that both transformer wires had to be connected to the track before we ever heard the terms "electrical circuit" or "continuity." We knew that the track had to be kept clean if the trains were to run well. We knew that car axles needed lubrication before we understood the physics of friction. We knew that if the spring inside the boxcar came out of its slot, the little man wouldn't pop out of the door, and that the nut on the contactor needed occasional adjustment to make the crossing gate operate correctly.

We didn't need to understand the theory of electric motors to free a sticking brush—we just had to know how to poke it with a toothpick. We knew how to fix many train things by applying simple logic to experience. That encouraged experimentation and made us fearless.

Later on, in high school (or some other such fool place) we were told that we had to understand *why* something worked before we could understand *how* to repair it. Like so many of the pontifications of well-intentioned academics, this new "knowledge" had a chilling effect. Unless we had a background in electromagnetic theory and understood why the armature rotated between the pole pieces, we had no business trying to fix an electric motor.

How ominous. How lucky we must have been as children to have gotten away with it. Better not try it now, we might fail. Adults must not fail in our society. Play it safe. If the train doesn't work, put it on the shelf and rationalize by calling it a "collectible."

I hear a lot of variations on this theme—anxiety-ridden adults, afraid to touch a repair project they would have tackled in a minute when they were twelve. Come on, guys, these are *toy trains* we're talking about. What's the worst that could happen? The thing doesn't work now, so what's the difference?

How complicated can it be to clean a commutator face, repair a broken wire, or replace worn pick-up shoes? You don't need an engineering degree to free a sticking motor brush—only a toothpick. (And a shot of TV tuner cleaner in the right place will prevent it from sticking again.) This additional dimension to your hobby can be a source of great satisfaction, even pride—the kind that comes with a challenge met and a job well done.

The focus of this book is on helping you keep your trains running and accessories working as they were intended. It deals with repair principles and service techniques that can be specifically or broadly applied and can be handled by almost anyone with common household tools and products. While it will show you *how* to perform maintenance and repairs in a practical way, you may also get to understand some of the theoretical *"whys"* about the technology in the process. In that case, so much the better.

I have tried to use straight English, avoiding as much technical language as possible. Although precise, the use of such terminology often gets in the way of clarity and understanding for us common folk. So, you don't have to be any kind of expert or even know the lingo to use this book.

What I offer here is a way of getting the job done. It may not be the only way, or even the best way, but it is a way. I learned train repair by doing it—by making mistakes and trying again. Eventually, I got the hang of it. You can too.

This book carries the theories and concepts I outlined in *Beginner's Guide to Repairing Lionel Trains* to the next level. Instead of limiting our service and maintenance to the externals, we will actually take the pieces apart to see what makes them tick and determine what might be wrong with them. We will use time-honored repair techniques and new parts, if necessary, in order to make them work again. Unless they were abused or badly butchered, most Lionel trains and accessories of any age can be resurrected and given a new lease on life.

(Note: A number of after-market toy train parts suppliers are in business across the country. They are a rich source of replacement parts and helpful information. All of them have mail-order lists. Many will take telephone orders. Some even have websites. Check out the ads in *Classic Toy Trains* magazine.)

You don't have to be any kind of expert or even know the lingo to use this book.

While only some of the more popular items from the so-called "classic" and "postwar" eras are used here as examples, all of the basic mechanisms are covered. The theories of repair can be successfully adapted to the newer and less common pieces. In fact, many of the old favorite Lionel pieces from the postwar era have been revived and rerun in recent years, using the original concepts and tooling. Only the colors and catalog numbers have been changed. Obviously, the repair techniques outlined here can be used with these new products as well.

However, the "can motor" and "circuit board" technologies employed by Lionel in recent years are a different matter. These things are not designed to be repaired in the field, at least by traditional means. As with the electronic components used in a wide variety of other products, faulty units are simply replaced by the company. This might seem wasteful, but such subassemblies have proven to be quite reliable. If they don't malfunction during the first few hours of use, they will last indefinitely. So, the lesson is this: Give your new equipment a real workout while it is still under warranty. If it fails, take it to your nearest Lionel authorized service station.

Lionel is the only toy company I know of with a string of such service stations stretching from coast to coast. Joshua Lionel Cowen took great pride in the reliability and durability of his products and set up a network of neighborhood repair facilities to keep them running. That tradition continues.

There never was a formal training program for Lionel service technicians. Most of them learned their trade on the job and by discussing repair techniques with their colleagues. New York service manager Irving Shull encouraged independent problem-solving and the open sharing of information among his employees. That set the tone for the other service stations. They were all provided with official service manuals and parts lists. Beyond that, they were on their own. Repair methods were learned through self-instruction, observation, or word of mouth from one technician to another.

In that great tradition, many of the hints and techniques in this book come from my own experiences and those of my colleagues in train repair and restoration. However, they are not just "off the top of our heads"; they also fall within the guidelines and suggestions contained in the Lionel service manuals.

So, in the spirit of sharing, I hope that what I may have learned over the years will be helpful to you and that you will in turn pass along whatever you learn to the next person.

We're all in the same gondola!

Let's get started. . . .

Repairing Lionel Locomotives

This section deals with keeping Lionel locomotives running. While steamers are used in the photos, the theories of repair in the first two sections (Universal motors and E-units) can be applied to diesels equally well.

Lionel also used two types of cheaper motors in some of their lower-end engines toward the end of the postwar era. They are the split-field models, which utilized a two-position reverse unit (no neutral mode), and the infamous "Scout" motors, characterized by their Bakelite cases and generally poor performance records. Repair methods for these are somewhat different. Since most serious operators rarely run these kinds of locos, they are not covered here.

The Lionel AC-DC "Universal Motors"

These reliable little motors were developed before World War I and became the workhorses of the Lionel fleet for over 70 years. When the new "can motor" technology began taking over a decade or so ago, they were slowly phased out.

Built in a variety of different sizes and configurations over the years, the basic Universal Motor concepts and electrical principles remained constant. They were designed to be very adaptable, finding their way into steam and diesel locomotives alike.

They also proved to be quite durable, requiring little maintenance except for regular lubrication and occasional cleaning. When repairs were necessary, they could usually be made with ordinary household tools.

Universal Motors had only three basic component subassemblies—the field, the armature, and the brush holder, all of which were replaceable. So, the little motors kept on going, and going, and going. . . .

The Lionel Sequence Reverse Units

Known generally from the outset as "E-Units," these devices also became a Lionel mainstay and tradition for over half a century. With the advent of can motors, the old electromechanical E-units were replaced by electronic circuit boards that did essentially the same thing.

The E-units provided a three-position sequence—"forward, neutral, reverse, neutral, etc." that was operationally desirable. Trains could be made to wait in neutral on busy layouts until the traffic had cleared and they were given a green light. This neutral mode was also important for some operating cars and trackside accessories.

Essentially solenoid-operated rotary switches, E-units were often the source of annoying trouble, due to dirty or worn contact fingers and early plastic rotary drums that tended to shrivel with age and drop out of place. Notoriously tricky to service—or to get back together after service—E-units became a constant frustration for technicians who were born with only two hands, when they tried to hold everything in place during reassembly.

An entire litany of incantations, oaths, and epithets grew up among those who regularly repaired these cantankerous devices. One old-timer told me that he used expletives in several languages—the one in Norwegian, evoking the wrath of Thor, seemed to be the most effective. Whatever works.

The Lionel Postwar Smoke Units

Rarely are postwar Lionel smoke units found in a condition that does not require some service. Often they are clogged with a hard, white residue from unexpended smoke pellets. Many young engineers over-fed their iron horses in an attempt to make them produce as much white smoke as the locomotives in the touched-up catalog pictures. Obviously, it didn't work; it just clogged up the unit. Sometimes, the heater coil is also found burned out or broken.

In both instances, I recommend converting the locomotive for use with the new smoke fluid. This stuff is more efficient, and the old smoke pellets are becoming harder and harder to find.

The Lionel Air Whistles

Most contemporary steam locomotive models employ digital audio systems that play back the recorded sounds of the real thing—wonderful technology and a very realistic effect. But there was a compelling charm about the sound of the old Lionel air-chime whistle that ruled the tinplate rails for 40 years—particularly when the impeller motor kicked in and started to rev up. To me, that sound is more in keeping with the whimsical world of toy trains.

Many of these old air whistles can be rejuvenated by a simple cleaning and lubrication. The tended to be neglected, if not totally overlooked, because they were built into the locomotive tenders.

Since many accessories, in addition to locomotives, use a version of Lionel's basic motor, you'll undoubtedly want to read this chapter closely.

PROJECT 1

Lionel Motors

This section covers basic maintenance and repair for traditional Lionel steam locomotives. Most of the principles can be applied to diesel locomotives and to trains made by other manufacturers as well.

We start with the heart of the locomotive, the motor itself. In subsequent chapters, we will cover E-unit sequence reversing mechanisms, smoke generators, and whistles.

If you have a post-1969 production steamer with a can motor and electronic circuit boards for reversing and sound effects, these principles and techniques will not be applicable. Like many things produced in today's world, those components are designed to be replaced, not repaired, when they stop working.

Components

Most of the electric motors used in toy trains—steam and diesel—have the same basic three elements (see fig. 1):

• A stationary *field*. This stack of thin steel plates shaped like a horseshoe is surrounded by many turns of enamel-coated copper wire. This combined assembly is known as the *field coil*.

• A three-pole *armature*. Another stack of steel plates on a shaft, this assembly spins around within the stationary field. Three coils of enamel-coated wire are wrapped around this stack. Each terminates as a wedge-shaped copper segment on the face of the armature, called a *pole piece*. The three pole pieces together form a circle known as the *commutator*.

• Two *brushes*. Usually made of copper-graphite, these little cylinders contact the commutator's surface. They are held firmly in place within individual *brush wells* by spring pressure.

How It All Works

When electricity flows into the field coil, the field turns into an electromagnet, the ends of which attract and repel simultaneously. Due to its horseshoe shape, the attract/repel forces are focused close together at the end of the field. The brushes are wired in series with the field so electrical current flows through them and into the armature at the same time. These attract/repel forces cause the armature coil (positioned between the ends of the field) to move out of the way. When it does, another coil automatically moves into position. It must also move out of the way, and as it does, a third comes into place. Soon the armature is spinning rapidly.

A typical toy train motor can develop as many as 4,000 rpm. It makes sense that anything revolving as fast as an armature will require a little attention from time to time. The following routine maintenance should be performed on the armature on a regular

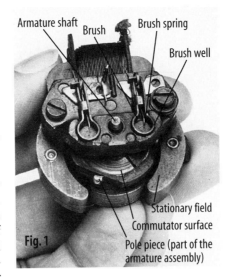

Fig. 1

Armature shaft Brush Brush spring Brush well Stationary field Commutator surface Pole piece (part of the armature assembly)

basis—after each hour of running time or whenever needed.

Lubrication

Start by oiling both ends of the armature shaft if they are accessible. See fig. 2. (It's okay to oil just the exposed end—the unexposed end rides in a lubricant-filled reservoir.) Use just one drop of oil, dispensed on the end of a toothpick. Don't apply too much.

Cleaning

Generally speaking, you can clean your motor without taking the locomotive apart. Begin with TV tuner cleaner, mineral spirits, or even rubbing alcohol. Spray down the commutator surface. Take another toothpick and clean out the three slots between the commutator segments (fig. 3). Use a cotton swab and wipe down the commutator surface, repeating until it shines and the swabs no longer turn black. See fig. 4.

While you're at it, lubricate the locomotive drive train too. This is the arrangement that transmits the motor's momentum to the drive wheels. On most locomotives it consists of either a series of spur gears or a worm and wheel. And don't forget the axles. A greasy lubricant works best on gears. (There are many good ones for toy train use. Shop around.) See fig. 5.

Simple routine maintenance will keep your locomotive's motor from arcing severely and running hot, thus lessening the danger of armature windings shorting or burning out. And your train will run better too!

Teardown

But there comes a time when routine maintenance just isn't enough and a complete cleaning and overhaul is needed. Start with motor removal.

• **Remove the motor mechanism from the locomotive body.**

Fig. 2. Oil the locomotive, using small amounts of oil dispensed onto the end of a toothpick.

Fig. 3. Use a toothpick to clean out the gaps on the commutator face. Start by spraying the face with TV tuner cleaner—that makes removing the dirt inside the gaps much easier.

Fig. 4. Clean the commutator face with swabs and TV tuner cleaner until the swabs no longer turn black. Dirt is a great insulator—not what you want here!

Fig. 5. (Above) A lubricated drive train increases gear life and puts less strain on the motor. Make sure you lubricate both gears and axles. **Fig. 6. (Above right)** An old Lionel motor is usually a dirty motor. Work cleaning solvent into the entire motor assembly using an old paintbrush until it's entirely clean. Be sure you lubricate both gears and axles afterwards.

How this is done depends on the type of steamer. It's a good idea to remove the front and rear trucks and to disconnect the valve gear, rod, and crosshead assemblies first. Then separate the mechanism from the die-cast body.

Many spur gear mechanisms are attached with a vertical screw through the top of the boiler and a transverse screw pin running through the front or back of the motor side plates. Others, notably those with worm drive, are joined to the boiler by screws through the bottom plate. Work slowly and carefully. Don't force anything.

• **Thoroughly clean the mechanism inside and out.** Remove the dust, dirt, and caked-on grease by washing everything in a bath of mineral spirits. You can either dip the mechanism or apply the solvent with an old paintbrush (fig. 6). Get into every crack and corner, working the dirt loose with the brush. Continue until the entire mechanism is clean. Allow the motor to air-dry completely.

(CAUTION: Mineral spirits is a very combustible liquid. Use only in a well-ventilated area, away from spark or flames. Some people only use it outdoors—that's a good idea.)

• **Test-run the mechanism.** A thorough cleaning will sometimes eliminate many of the gremlins. Before you run the motor, make sure everything has dried. Carefully and sparingly lubricate all bearings first. The mineral spirits bath removes all traces of lubricant. If you don't lubricate before operation, you'll learn firsthand what "squeaky clean" really means!

• **Remove the brushplate and brushes.** Remove the two or three screws that secure the plate. Be careful you don't lose the brushes and the brush springs—they jump! Set them aside temporarily.

• **Test the armature for shorts and open windings.** This is particularly important if your locomotive has been running erratically, noisily, or even just

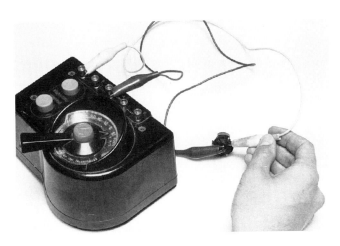 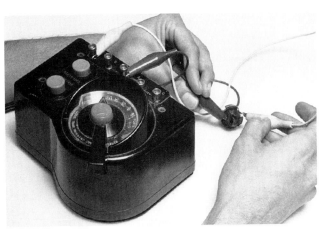

Fig 7. Erratic operation usually indicates open motor windings or even a short-circuited armature. If you touch one transformer lead to the armature shaft and the other to a commutator segment, there shouldn't be a spark.

Fig. 8. Continuity should occur between commutator segments. Hold one transformer lead to one segment, and touch the other lead to one of the two remaining segments. It should spark. No sparking (or no needle jump on a voltammeter) indicates no continuity between the segments.

slowly. There *should be continuity* between the segments of the commutator face and *no continuity* between the commutator segments and the armature shaft.

Testing is easy if you have a volt-ohm-milliammeter or another simple continuity tester. If you don't have one, you can use the leads from your transformer. Turn the throttle to middle range. Touch one lead to the armature shaft and the other to one of the commutator segments. There should be no spark generated. Repeat this test with the other two commutator segments. See fig. 7.

If sparking occurs, the armature is shorted against the shaft and must be rewound or replaced. (Since motor rewinding is a highly technical specialty, it's beyond the scope of this chapter. It may be cheaper and easier to replace the armature with a good used one.)

Next, touch one of the transformer leads to one of the commutator segments. Then touch the other lead wire to the other two commutator segments in turn. There should be a small spark produced here. Go around the commutator and test each segment against the other two. There should be a spark each time. No spark indicates a break in the continuity, an open circuit (fig. 8).

You may have to rewind or replace the armature. Your only

hope is that the coil wire has just broken loose from its anchor on the commutator face. If you're lucky, the wire will be long enough, and you can resolder it back in place.

• **Clean and dress the commutator face.** Chances are good that TV tuner cleaner and cotton swabs will be all you'll need. As explained in the section on cleaning, spray the tuner cleaner directly into the commutator face and swab until the surface is shiny and clean (fig. 4). Use a toothpick to remove any gunk between the commutator segments.

In extreme cases where the commutator face is severely worn, pitted, or has circular grooves cut into the surface, dress (lightly sand) it with fine emery paper until all evidence of grooving and pitting is gone. You should see no more black rings or marks, but instead just a clean copper surface.

• **Clean, repair, or replace the brushes and springs.** There are two sides to the ongoing "brush replacement controversy." Some service technicians replace brushes and springs every time a motor is taken apart. Others believe in conservation, stretching and bending the brush springs until only a nub of copper-graphite cylinder is left. It's up to you.

Regardless of your position in this debate, brushes should be

replaced when they're so short that the brush wells can no longer hold them firmly in place (they "wobble" from side to side). Brushes should fit snugly within the brush wells, but there should be no binding to inhibit their free "in-and-out" movement as they ride on the commutator face.

That's why it's important that the wells be thoroughly cleaned. Spray the insides with tuner cleaner, and follow up with a cotton swab (or pipe cleaner in the smaller-diameter wells) until all traces of dirt are removed. Unless the brushplate is warped, this is all the maintenance this assembly will need (fig. 9).

Clean the brushes with tuner cleaner or mineral spirits. Wipe away all the black residue from the sides and ends. They were originally a dark copper color and should appear that way again after cleaning.

If the brushes have worn into a lopsided angle (their end profile is not perpendicular to the sides), they should be squared off by gently rubbing them over emery paper or a fine file. This will assure maximum contact between brushes and commutator.

I can already hear someone saying, "Replace them! Lopsided wear indicates the brushes are too short!" I prefer to square them first and, if they wear that way again,

11

Fig 9. (Left) Like other parts of the motor, the brush wells need to be cleaned. Use TV tuner cleaner and cotton swabs. **(Center)** Do the same for the brushes while they're out of the wells. They should have a dark copper finish after cleaning. **Fig. 10. (Right)** Adjusting brush spring tension is easy. Clamp the motor to a board so the wheels can operate freely while still allowing you to put pressure on the brushes. Using a toothpick, push on the brushes while the motor is running. If the motor speeds up, the springs are too weak. Adjust accordingly.

then replace them. Remember, we live in a world of finite resources—just ask your local service station. (And now you know my position in the replacement controversy!)

Such wear can also be the result of a warped brushplate or brush holders that are too loose, or it may simply indicate that the locomotive was run more in one direction than the other.

• **Check the spring tension.** In most cases, little or nothing will need to be done to brush springs. If there's evidence of uneven tension, such as a difference in brush length or the locomotive running faster in one direction than the other, you'll have to adjust or replace your springs. Tension should be equal on both brushes.

The problem in diagnosing improper spring tension is that either too much or too little can sometimes result in the same symptom—a motor loses power or runs slower than it should.

Too much tension is rarely encountered, except in cases where the motor has previously been "repaired" by someone who didn't

quite get it right. Too little tension is often the result of brushes shortened by excessive wear or springs that have lost their resiliency. This is common with coil springs that have been overheated.

• **Adjust the spring tension.** This operation can be tricky and requires patience because it's done by trial and error. This is why many service technicians routinely replace brushes and springs every time they overhaul an engine. That eliminates the need for adjustment in most cases. However, if no replacements are available, adjustment is the only option.

Start by clamping the motor to an upright board in a vise so that all wheels and gears can move freely. Hook transformer leads to one of the third-rail pickups and one of the motor side plates. Turn the throttle up about halfway.

With the motor running, carefully poke a toothpick or a piece of wire into each brush well. Gently apply more brush pressure against the spinning commutator (fig. 10). If the motor speeds up,

the spring tension is too weak.

Adjust the coil springs by stretching them *slightly*. Flat or wire springs may be bent to exert more pressure. Be very careful, and stretch them only a little at a time. Repeat the toothpick test after each bending or stretching operation until the motor no longer speeds up when the brushes are prodded.

Too much tension can be detected by simply loosening the brushplate slightly. With the motor running, just loosen each brushplate screw by backing it off a half-turn at a time. If the motor speeds up appreciably, it may indicate that the spring tension is too great. (In addition, this can indicate a faulty or a worn brushplate bearing.)

Flat or wire springs may be bent back to relieve the tension. Coils may be shortened by snipping off a winding or two. Again, adjust the springs a little at a time. Repeat the test and adjustment until the motor runs at full rpm with the brushplate tight.

Running Again

Well, that takes care of overhauling the locomotive's motor. By this time, your engine should be running quite well, at least in one direction! We'll tackle directional problems when we discuss E-units in the next chapter.

What good is a train that runs in only one direction? Lionel's reversing mechanism, called an E-unit, is the key to good times when operating your train. Unfortunately, E-units can be balky and need regular attention.

PROJECT 2

Lionel E-units

The sequence reverse unit (also known as the "E-unit"), can be a source of trouble in older, high-mileage locomotives. When it was invented some 75 years ago, the E-unit was the wonder of the model train industry. Lionel bought Ives just to get the rights to it. Because it was so well-conceived from the start, the E-unit's basic design has changed very little over the years.

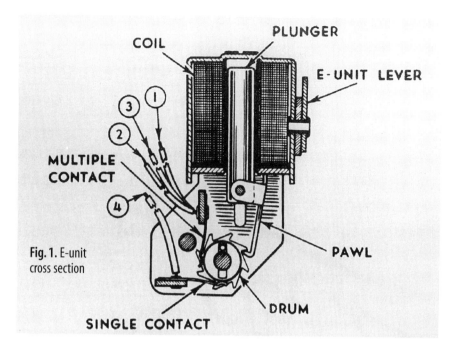

Fig. 1. E-unit cross section

COIL

PLUNGER

E-UNIT LEVER

MULTIPLE CONTACT

PAWL

DRUM

SINGLE CONTACT

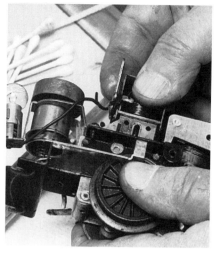

Fig. 2. (Above) Remove the screws holding the E-unit in place, and slowly pull it away from the engine's frame. If you're careful, you won't have to resolder the wiring back together.

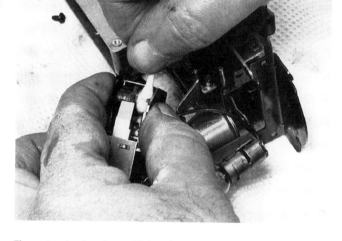

Fig. 3. (Above and right) Bathe the E-unit's drum in TV tuner cleaner, available from Radio Shack.

Then wipe the drum's metallic bands with cotton swabs until the bands shine once again.

What Is It?

An E-unit is a rotary, solenoid-operated double-throw switch, with an "off" position between the throws. Through its action, the E-unit changes the connections of the brushes in relation to the motor field, reversing the motor rotation direction and changing the direction of the locomotive. An E-unit consists of a coil, a plunger that's equipped with a hook-like pawl, a ratchet-toothed drum having electrical contact bands, and two sets of "finger" contacts. Everything is held within a sheet-metal framework inside most locomotives' frames (fig. 1). When track power is applied, the plunger rises and is held inside the coil. When the power is interrupted for any reason, the plunger automatically drops and the pawl engages the next tooth on the drum. When power is restored, the plunger rises into the coil and the pawl rotates the drum 45 degrees. This drum movement positions the finger contacts onto different drum contact bands, placing the motor into the next sequence mode. When kept clean and in good shape, the E-unit functions quite reliably, providing the familiar "forward-neutral-reverse-neutral-forward" sequence whenever the track power is interrupted. A faulty E-unit can be responsible for more problems than just reversing malfunctions. Worn or dirty contacts can produce excessive arcing, which leads to erratic or slow motor performance.

Cleaning

Because the E-unit is usually mounted close to motor bearings, gears, and other moving parts, it's susceptible to lubricant spatter and dirt. This is the major cause of E-unit trouble.

• **Remove the E-unit from the frame.** It's usually held in place by one or two screws. There should be enough slack to allow cleaning without disconnecting the wires (fig. 2).

• **Check the wires and finger contacts.** Make sure that the wires are soldered securely into place. Repair as needed. Perform a visual inspection of the six finger contacts. Bent or severely worn contacts are a common source of trouble.

• **Spray TV tuner cleaner onto the drum's surface.** See fig. 3. The spray loosens the accumulation of greasy residue. Mop it up with clean cotton swabs. Rotate the drum by hand, and continue the spray-and-mop operation until you've cleaned all the drum's metal contact bands. If the bands don't shine, keep cleaning until they do.

• **Check the lock-out.** Located on the front of the E-unit, the lock-out lever must make good contact when thrown into position. If necessary, carefully bend the lever's contact portion so that the dimple on its end seats firmly within the eyelet contact on the fiber strip. There should be no looseness between the eyelet and the lever's dimple.

• **Reinstall the E-unit.** Wait until all traces of the solvent have evaporated and then test-run the mechanism. Put it through the "forward-neutral-reverse-neutral-forward" cycle at least a dozen times. It often takes a few spins to get the freshly cleaned parts to "wear in" and work properly.

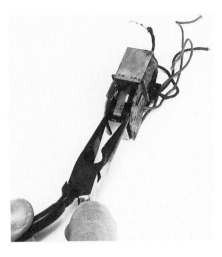

Fig. 4. Spread the E-unit's metal plates apart using needlenose pliers. Work carefully—and look out for flying parts

Overhaul

If your E-unit doesn't perform well after a good cleaning, it needs an overhaul. This is the point where many people throw up their hands. They've heard stories about how difficult E-units are to take apart and reassemble. I'll admit that it's a bit tricky and even a little frustrating, but it can be done. Be patient and work carefully.

• **Remove the E-unit again.** If you're lucky, you still may avoid disconnecting any wires, but look at it this way: If you're lucky enough to rebuild your E-unit you're probably lucky enough to rewire its connections.

• **Test the solenoid coil.** Touch your transformer leads to the solder lugs on both ends of the fiber strip (front area of the coil). You

should see and hear the plunger recede into the coil. If you don't, look for broken or loose wires leading from the coil to the lugs.

If a wire has broken loose of its terminal, resolder it into place. If it's broken in midsection (away from the terminal), splice an extension between the broken end and the solder lug. Remember, the coil wire is coated with enamel insulation. This has to be carefully removed with fine emery cloth or sandpaper before the wire can be attached or soldered to anything. Shorted or burned coils must be rewound or replaced.

• **Take the thing apart.** The recommended procedure involves spreading the side plates apart with a pair of pliers (fig. 4). At some point, one of the plates will suddenly let go and cause everything to fly apart.

• **Clean the solenoid.** The plunger and the sleeve within the coil need a TV tuner cleaner bath. Not realizing that these surfaces must not be lubricated, many service people have oiled or greased them; over time that lubrication dries out. Dried grease is the most common cause of sticking solenoids (fig. 5). If the tuner cleaner won't touch it, you may have to scrape or wire-wheel it off. The goal is completely free plunger movement.

• **Check the finger contacts.** They're usually worn and pitted. Any pits or narrowing of the metal near the fingertips indicates that

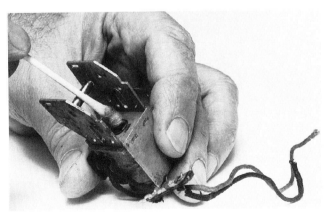

Fig. 5. (Above and right) Clean out the plunger tube and plunger with a cotton swab and more tuner cleaner.

That sticky, dirty mixture of old graphite, grease, and other lubrication can gum up an otherwise functional solenoid.

Fig. 6. Make sure the finger contacts are also clean. Use swabs and TV tuner cleaner.

Fig. 7. The old drum on the right is misshapen and the bands are pitted; it will keep an E-unit from properly sequencing.

the finger contacts should be replaced. Bend acceptable finger assemblies slightly to ensure firm contact with the drum when reinserted (fig. 6).

• **Examine the drum for shrinkage.** Early plastics weren't stable, and drums made from them have often distorted over time (fig. 7). Even a slight malformation will cause the drum to seat loosely, interfere with smooth rotation, and result in poor electrical contact. Buy a new one.

The drum should be perfectly cylindrical with tight metal contact bands. Inspect the ratchet teeth for chips, cracks, and wear. Examine the "land" between the metal bands for dents or furrows made by overheated contact fingers. Look for pits in the contacts. Check the drum ends for wear by inserting them into the side plate bearing holes. (The fit should be smooth,

with no slop or play.) Don't try to "fix" the drum in any way. If your drum isn't perfect, replace it.

• **Reassemble the E-unit.** Lionel service stations had special tools and jigs for this task, so don't be discouraged if you have to make several attempts before the thing goes together properly.

Take your time. Work logically. With the unit on its side, put the components into place one at a time. Start with the plunger/pawl assembly. Next comes the strip with the four contact fingers. Position it within the slots provided, and bring the side plates together close enough to hold everything in place.

With the side plates slightly spread apart, insert the drum into one bearing hole. (Check *now* that the drum is positioned correctly—the pawl should advance the ratchet, not slide over the teeth.)

Carefully insert the other finger contact strip into the lower slot.

Now, slowly squeeze the side plates together, keeping all components in their proper places as you proceed (fig. 8). Finish by tapping the end of the transverse mounting stud with a ball peen hammer to tighten the assembly.

• **Pawl adjustment.** Frequently the locomotive will go through the sequence perfectly, but then it will run briefly either backward or forward in neutral mode before stopping. This is common after E-unit overhaul, and a simple pawl-angle adjustment will do the trick. Just bend it (upward, usually) with needlenose pliers until the pawl rotates the drum correctly.

• **Reinstall the E-unit.** All that's left to do is to make certain that the E-unit's bare wires and solder joints are not touching the frame or the cab casting.

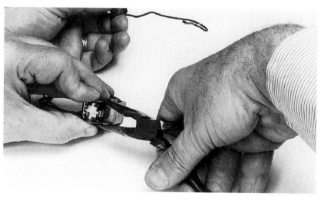

Fig. 8. (Above and right) After you've installed the solenoid/coil unit and the main finger assembly on the base plate, put the top plate in position and guide the drum into the bearing holes.

Crimp the two plates together with needlenose pliers. This is a job that may require a third hand. Since you probably have only two, this is a good opportunity to introduce a friend to the joy of toy train repair!

Old smoke units, relying on pellets for which you'll pay top collector dollar, are better replaced by units that work better and use inexpensive, readily available smoke fluid.

PROJECT 3

Converting Lionel Smoke Units

Real smoke. It was big news in Lionel's 1946 train line. No previous feature had been given quite as much hype. Even though Lionel's first smoking locomotives weren't as successful as the advertising trumpeted, the improved 1947 smoke generator design lasted with only minor changes until 1969.

Lionel smoke units use little white pellets (known as "SP," or smoke pellets, on the bottle). After a single pellet is dropped down a locomotive's smokestack, the heating element melts the pill and produces a white vapor with a distinct aroma. A piston connected to the locomotives drive train pumps air through a tiny hole in the bottom of the chamber, causing the puffing effect. Lionel made some changes to piston linkages and smoke unit mounting brackets during the postwar years, but the coil heaters and smoke chambers remained the same (fig. 1).

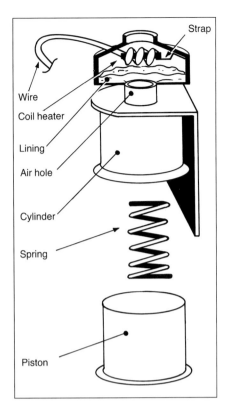

Fig. 1. Lionel smoke unit

Fig. 2. Most dealers and service stations stock these smoke unit conversion parts.

Making Smoke from Pills

Most catalog illustrations from that time show locomotives with clouds of smoke billowing from their stacks. At their best, original Lionel smoke generators produce more of a wisp than a billow. This discrepancy between catalog depiction and reality is why so many smoke units suffered fatal pill overdoses at the hands of enthusiastic young engineers.

Smoke generators work well if operated within the recommended instruction book guidelines—one pill at a time. But most kids didn't pay much attention to the instructions and operated on the assump-

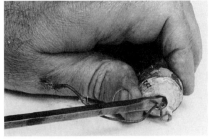

Fig. 3. After scoring the sealed joint with a hobby knife, pry the old smoke unit cap off with a screwdriver.

tion that if one pill was good, two (or three, or four) would be better.

Lionel heater coils are designed to handle only one pill at a time. Adding more only serves to cool the heater element, actually producing less smoke. Between operating sessions, the liquefied pellets harden in the bottom of the chamber, clogging the air hole and disabling the puffing feature. That liquefied material has also been known to drip through the hole and freeze the piston to the cylinder walls.

More daring kids soon discovered that if they parked the locomotive in neutral and turned up the voltage for a few minutes, they could melt the hardened residue and get the train to puff again. This worked, but it also drastically shortened the heater coil's life. That is why so many smoking postwar locomotives are found with burned-out coils or hopelessly clogged chambers.

Fig. 4. Scrape out the excess smoke pellet residue. You may need to heat the chamber and liquefy the residue to remove it.

If you're a collector and are hung up on original parts and condition, you'll have to live with a broken smoke generator or replace it with a costly, operational original. To make matters worse, original Lionel SP smoke pellets haven't been made in years and now enjoy collector status—with collector prices to match.

If you enjoy operating your trains and want a locomotive that puffs as it should, Lionel offers a solution—conversion. You can buy a small number of parts that will convert your old pill-type smoke unit to smoke fluid operation (fig. 2), at a cost of about $5. And it will smoke better than it ever did with pellets.

How to Do It

Conversion is simple. If your piston and linkage aren't covered with pill residue and still operate freely, you may not even have to remove the smoke unit from the

Fig. 5. Place the new lining material into the bottom of the chamber casting. It's important to make sure that the air hole isn't covered by the material.

Fig. 6. (Left) Align the heater element directly under the plastic cap's filler hole. **(Below)** Now press-fit the heater element onto the chamber casting. Make certain it doesn't obstruct the air hole in the casting.

Fig. 7. (Left) After installing heat-shrink tubing on both leads, attach one wire to the E-unit "hot" terminal. **(Above)** Attach the other to a ground location. Reinstall the shell, and test your new smoke unit.

locomotive chassis. Start by removing the boiler shell.

• **Remove the smoke unit cover.** Break the old cement joint around the top edge of the unit by scribing it with an X-acto knife. Use a screwdriver and pry the cover off (fig. 3).

• **Remove the old material.** This includes the old heater coil element as well as the smoke unit lining. We'll eventually replace both.

• **Remove all pill residue.** You can usually scrape it out (fig. 4). In extreme cases, the unit will have to be heated and the liquefied residue removed with cotton swabs.

• **Insert the new lining material.** Place it on the bottom of the chamber casting. Be sure the air hole remains unobstructed (fig. 5).

• **Center the heating element.**

In most cases I've used conversion elements that are already centered in the new plastic cover. If yours isn't centered, do so now and bend the lead wires to keep it in position (fig. 6).

• **Install the new cover.** Make sure the heater element is still centered and attached, and snap the cover onto the chamber casting. (The cap is a press-fit, so don't glue it into place.) It doesn't matter how the cap is positioned. Just be sure the heating element on the cap underside doesn't interfere with the air hole.

• **Insulate the new wires.** Install heat-shrink tubing over the exposed wires, and heat into place.

• **Attach the wires.** Attach one wire to the E-unit lug where the old smoke unit wire had been connected. Ground the other wire to a convenient screw on the locomotive's frame (fig. 7).

• **Test the unit.** Put two drops of smoke fluid (any brand will do) directly on the heater element. Attach transformer leads to the locomotive and apply power. If you've done everything correctly, the reconditioned smoke generator should work almost immediately.

• **Finish up.** Install the new gasket over the cover hole, and reinsert the mechanism into the locomotive boiler casting. Make sure the smoke unit's hole and the smokestack hole in the shell line up before you complete the reassembly. Adjust if necessary.

By now you should have a smooth-running, correctly reversing, smokin' engine!

A favorite of J.L. Cowen, his steam-engine whistles do a good job of mimicking the haunting sound of the real thing.

PROJECT 4

Lionel Whistles

The deep-throated, two-tone air chime whistle was Joshua Lionel Cowen's pride and joy. He invested much in its development, tuning the high and low resonating chambers until they reverberated a blend of sounds that he considered to be the miniature equivalent of those produced by prototype steam hotshots of the day.

Lionel's was the first whistle to be housed within a moving train, and it could be blown remotely at the operator's will with the touch of a button. Its sound fit well amid the out-of-scale rolling stock and three-rail track of Tinplate Land. Lionel produced the whistle in large quantities with only minor changes throughout the postwar era.

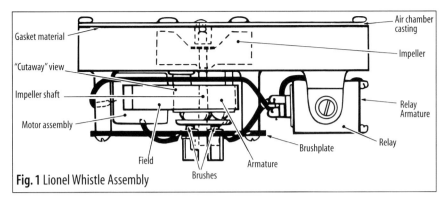

Fig. 1 Lionel Whistle Assembly

Gasket material
"Cutaway" view
Impeller shaft
Motor assembly
Field
Brushes
Armature
Brushplate
Relay
Relay Armature
Impeller
Air chamber casting

Fig. 2. The first places to check on a malfunctioning whistle tender are the two roller pickup assemblies. The whistle's wires should be in good condition and firmly soldered to the pickups' contacts. The two pickup springs should also exert enough pressure to keep the rollers in contact with the railhead. The pickups could probably stand a TV tuner bath too.

Fig. 3. Malfunctioning relays are common reasons for whistles not working. Test a relay by touching transformer leads to each of its terminals and pressing the whistle button. If the armature lifts slightly (but the contact points still don't touch one another), try bending the pivot points slightly to loosen things up. If nothing happens, get a new relay.

Cowen's whistle was an ingenious device for its day (fig. 1). A surge of direct current superimposed over the alternating current track voltage causes a coil relay in the tender to close, energizing the whistle motor. Impeller blades on the motor's shaft whip up the air, forcing it against the openings in the air chamber and producing the sound.

Problems

Lionel whistles were mounted inside tenders, which made them relatively inaccessible. As a result, most never received adequate lubrication and maintenance. As bearings dried out and commutators became clogged with dirt, the level of motor noise increased. In extreme cases, whistle bearings can become so dry that the only sounds they produce resemble the squealing of a small pig with its tail caught in a barn door. (This shouldn't be confused with the normal "oink oink" intonations emitted by Lionel diesel horns.)

Don't let all of this worry you. Unless there's structural damage to the whistle chamber or the motor bearings are severely worn, most Lionel whistles can be brought back to life quite easily.

Clean and Repair

• **Test your whistle controller.** Critical parts inside the controller deteriorate with age. The easiest way to test it is with another whistle tender that you know functions properly. If the functional whistle doesn't work, go ahead and replace your controller.

• **Check electrical connections.** Make sure the solder joints on the wires between the whistle and rail roller pickups are tight (fig. 2). Also check the third-rail roller pickup—it must exert sufficient pressure on the railhead to energize the whistle unit. Clean the roller pickup by spraying it with TV tuner cleaner and wiping with a cotton swab or cloth.

• **Remove the tender shell.** It's usually held in place by screws or a combination of screws and tabs. Remove the screws and bend the tabs carefully.

• **Check for broken wires.** Look over all exposed wiring on the whistle unit for broken, shorted, or poorly soldered connections. Repair as needed.

• **Test the relay.** If it doesn't respond at all, the coil may be burned out or shorted. In that case, replacement is the solution. However, if the armature does lift slightly (but not enough to close the contact points), adjustment at the pivot points is probably necessary. Minor bending of the pivot points will often free the action or lessen the tension, allowing the relay to close easily (fig. 3).

• **Clean and tune.** Like your locomotive's motor, the whistle motor needs a good cleaning. Use the techniques and products described in "Repairing Lionel motors." Clean the brush wells, brushes, and commutator face with TV tuner cleaner. Remove debris from the commutator slots, and dress the commutator face with emery paper. Test the field coil and armature windings for shorted or open circuits (fig. 4).

• **Lubricate the motor shaft bearings.** I begin with light oil, letting it soak into very dry bearings. Then I run the motor at top speed for about a minute. This should take care of bearing chatter and squeal. If it doesn't, repeat the process.

Don't forget to mop up any oil that may have splattered about during the high-speed running. Then finish by greasing the bearings for more lasting lubrication.

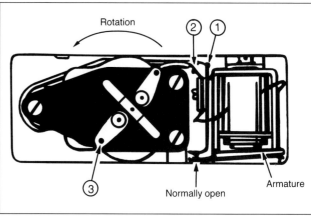

Fig. 4. This commutator face has seen better days. Clean it with TV tuner cleaner, cotton swabs, and toothpicks, using the same methods used for cleaning Lionel motors (see Chapter 1). Also, test the commutator segments for continuity, and clean the brushes and brush wells.

Fig. 5. Sometimes the last "service person" to monkey with a whistle managed to get the wires reversed. Take a good look at this illustration and then examine your whistle assembly. Are the wires contacting points 1, 2, and 3 in the correct position?

Oh, and don't wear your favorite shirt during this step. Did I mention this too late?

If the motor is still noisy after cleaning and lubrication, the problem may be severely worn bearings. Worn bearings come from repeated whistle use without proper lubrication. I've seen whistle bearings so badly distorted that the armature actually rubs against the field during "operation," if it can be called that. In this case, the only cure is new bearings.

Action Without Sound

What if your motor runs great and responds faithfully to the whistle controller, but there's still little or no sound? Here are four possible reasons and what to do about them:

• **The motor spins in the wrong direction.** Yes, it's true. This problem generally signals an earlier "fix" job that succeeded in reassembling the whistle incorrectly. Lionel whistle motors are supposed to run counterclockwise when viewed from the perspective of the brushplate. Be sure the wires are connected as shown in fig. 5.

• **Broken or malfunctioning impeller blades.** The impeller blades inside the whistle unit may be broken, or the impeller itself may be slipping on its shaft. If the

blades are broken, the entire impeller should be replaced. Try your local swap meet and discover faith. In the case of slippage, a judicious application of epoxy cement or gel-type super glue in the right places can often correct the problem.

• **The air chamber leaks.** Diecast air chambers were put together with a gasket material that dries out and shrinks with age. This causes air leaks at the seams. The later, all-plastic air chambers also occasionally suffer from cracks at the seams and elsewhere.

I've had good results sealing these leaks with a household cement like Duco. Small cracks may be filled directly. A bead of cement around the gasket joints on the older chambers will usually do the job. For plastic chambers, try gluing small styrene patches over the leaks, using Testor's or Tenax liquid cement (fig. 6).

• **The air chamber is clogged.** This is fairly rare, tending to happen with trains that lived in homes decorated with shag carpet. The rotating impeller blades act like a little vacuum cleaner, inhaling lint, fuzz, and pet hair. Once I even found a cocoon inside a whistle chamber.

The older die-cast whistle units can—and should—be taken apart

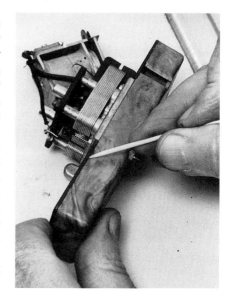

Fig. 6. It's common for aging Lionel die-cast air chamber gaskets to spring a leak. Use household cement to fill the gap between the two air chamber castings, then reassemble the halves. Later whistle tenders contain plastic chambers. They're easily sealed by using Testor's or Tenax liquid cement and small styrene patches.

for cleaning. Unfortunately, the later plastic ones don't come apart as easily. The only thing I can suggest with plastic units is to blow out the obstruction with an air hose. If that doesn't work, get creative or find another chamber. This concludes our dissertation on Lionel locomotive repair.

Repairing Switches, Controllers, and Couplers

These are the unsung heroes of Lionel railroading. They aren't a flashy streamliner, making up time at 120 per as it roars across the miles between Lionelville and Lionel City. They aren't a peddler freight, poking along, picking up and dropping off cars along the way. They aren't even switch engines, patrolling the yards, making up trains for the waiting road locomotives to carry off to all parts. They don't load or unload raw materials, commodities, or livestock or warn passing motorists of approaching trains.

In short, nobody notices them. They are supposed to perform a role in support of the more glamorous side of the railroad. They are taken for granted. But without any of them operating efficiently, the Lionel lines would grind to a standstill.

Lionel's 022 switches were the standard that existed unchanged for over half a century, because of their durability and reliability.

The Lionel knuckle coupler, although it was "improved" a number of times over essentially the same period, remains a constant. Other toy train manufacturers use it as the prototype for their own coupler design. All are compatible with it.

Lionel accessories have always been ingenious in their concept, function, and operation, but they cannot perform without their controllers.

In this chapter, we will show you how to keep your switches snapping smartly and your couplers in good operational repair. Because they are often missing, we will also provide guidelines on making your own controllers for the more popular Lionel accessories, using readily available component parts from Radio Shack or other such electronics supply stores.

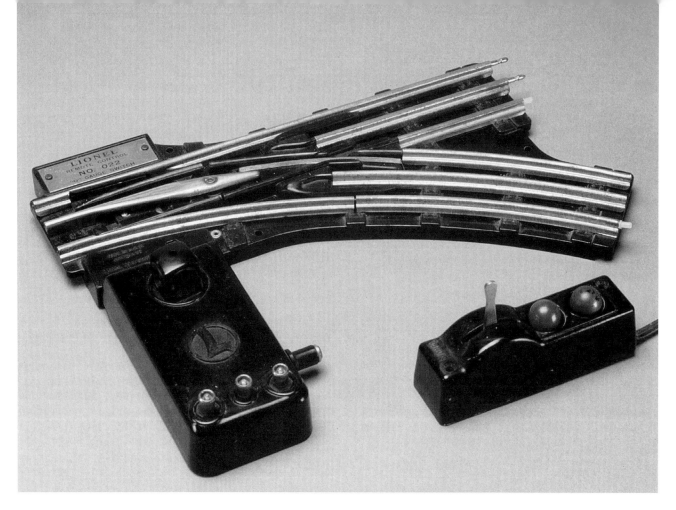

Remote-control, nonderailing switches were usually the next in line following purchase of the Christmas morning train set. They're marvelous pieces of electrical ingenuity and found on nearly every Lionel layout. Surprisingly, they're very reliable and not difficult to repair.

PROJECT 5

022 Switches

Legendary for their design and performance, Lionel's no. 022 switches were manu-factured from the late 1930s to the late 1960s. Revived and renumbered 5132/33 in 1980, these "old reliables" were again available for another 14 years. They remain the choice of most operators, with good reason—they're high-quality pieces. Because they're complex, problems occasionally arise, but thankfully they're simple to repair.

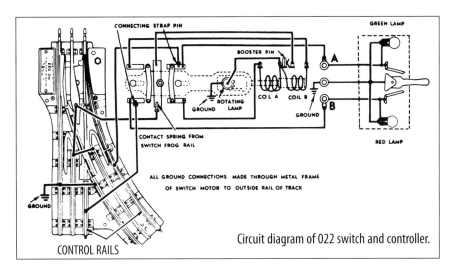

CONNECTING STRAP PIN

GREEN LAMP

BOOSTER PIN

A

ROTATING LAMP

GROUND

COIL A   COIL B

GROUND

B

RED LAMP

CONTACT SPRING FROM
SWITCH FROG RAIL

ALL GROUND CONNECTIONS MADE THROUGH METAL FRAME
OF SWITCH MOTOR TO OUTSIDE RAIL OF TRACK

GROUND

CONTROL RAILS

Circuit diagram of 022 switch and controller.

Heavy-Duty Performers

Built to take the stresses of heavy-duty use, the 022s (it is not O-22, by the way) feature solid, precise, and labor-intensive construction. They have many, many moving parts: Much can go wrong, but usually doesn't, as long as they're kept clean and well maintained. (Lionel O-72 switches share many parts, including their mechanisms, so most of these repair tips apply to them as well. The post-1993 no. 23010/11 "O31" O gauge switches are a new design, though, and do not share parts with 022s.)

The 022 mechanism, or "switch motor," utilizes a double solenoid, two coils wound around a common tube. The plunger is linked mechanically to the switch mechanism (fig. 1).

Power for the switch motor and the controller lamps can be obtained directly from the track layout through the third rail or via a special plug on the side of the motor case (used when operating 022s on a fixed voltage). See fig. 2. Inserting the plug automatically disconnects the track power supply to the switch. Over the years, most operators have opted to use the fixed-voltage feature, because the switches simply work better on a steady supply of 16 volts or more. (I like to use 18 to 20 volts on my layout—the switches really snap.)

A diagram of the switch motor and controller circuit is shown above. As it illustrates, the swivel rails have two positions. In the position illustrated, the rails are set for the train to run along the straight branch of the switch.

Note that the moving contacts are set so that the power is routed through terminal A to energize the green lamp on the controller. With the swivel rails in the curved position, power would be routed through terminal B and the red light would go on.

The 022 switches have a feature, called "nonderailing," that automatically throws the swivel rails to the proper alignment and allows the train to pass smoothly through the switch. This is accomplished via the two insulated control rails shown in the diagram. If the train approaches an open switch, its wheels, passing over the control rail, complete the electrical circuit that throws the switch. (Always remember to place insulating pins in the control rails when placing a 022 or other nonderailing switch on your layout.)

As you can see, in addition to moving the swivel rails, the double solenoid in the switch motor also rotates the illuminated switch lantern and moves the two sets of contacts that allow the switch to be thrown remotely, while selecting the correct colored lamp on the controller.

Testing the 022

All electrical connections between the switch motor and the switch itself are made by pressure contacts. Two pins mate with corresponding contacts on the

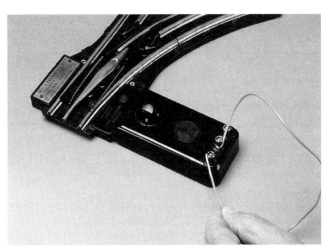

Fig. 1. While applying power to the switch rails, use a jumper wire between the terminals to check the solenoid for proper operation.

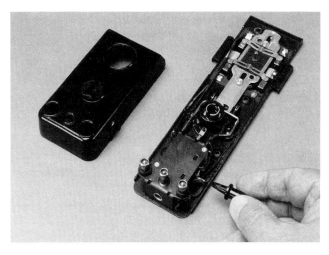

Fig. 2. The fixed-voltage feature of the Lionel 022 allows you to power your switches from a separate power supply.

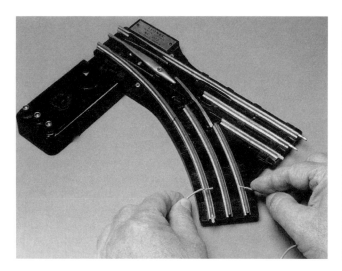

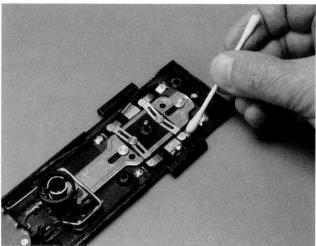

Fig. 3. (Above) Connecting the two outside rails with a jumper wire confirms whether the nonderailing feature is operating correctly.

Fig. 4. (Above right) Clean the contacts with a cotton swab moistened with tuner cleaner.

switch motor. One of them is riveted to the curved-side connection assembly and the other to the straight-side connection assembly. These pins, along with a contact spring projecting from the frog rail of the switch and a brass ground link at the back, must make good contact or the switch will not operate.

Test the operation of the switch by applying about 18 volts to the ends of the center and outside rails. The lantern bulb should go on. Attach a short piece of wire to the center binding post on the switch motor. Touch the other end of the wire to each of the outside binding posts in turn. The swivel rails should move smartly back and forth. Next, test the nonderailing feature by bridging your short wire between each of the control rails and the running rail opposite to it. The swivel rails should move correspondingly (fig. 3).

The swivel rails should lock securely in both positions. If they don't, check the hinge lock assembly. If it's not broken or out of place, you can adjust the front of the wire bar by bending it slightly. A bent swivel pin rubbing against the slot, the lantern assembly rubbing against the switch cover, or

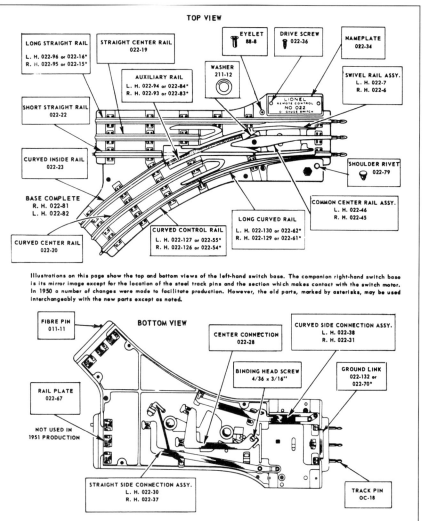

The 022 switch itself. Note the connecting straps.

some other mechanical interference—debris, a loose lamp bracket or lantern retainer pivot, or a wire in the way of the action—may also prevent the switch from locking.

If the switch doesn't work at all, check the continuity of the electrical circuits in the switch motor. Look for loose solder joints, broken wires, or a poor contact between

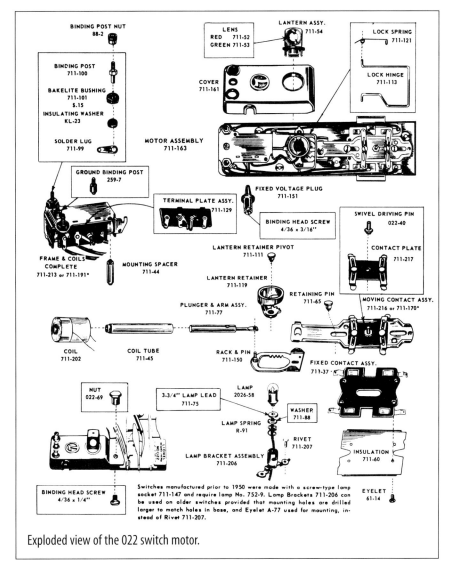

Fig. 5. Occasionally, the connections underneath the switch break. If that happens, simply solder the pieces back together.

Exploded view of the 022 switch motor.

the spring and booster pin in the fixed-voltage circuit. Check the continuity of both solenoid coils. Look for possible shorts: in the lamp socket, between the center rail and swivel pin, where solder lugs are touching the frame, or loose rivets in the binding posts.

If the switch works in one direction only, or irregularly in both, the trouble may lie in the sliding contact assembly. Check for loose riveting of the springs to their insulating base, and of the base to the rest of the assembly. Loose rivets may cause the parts to shift enough to miss making contact. Clean the contact surfaces with TV tuner cleaner or a cotton swab dipped in mineral spirits or alcohol (fig. 4). Check the tension on the springs to see that contact is made at all four points. Adjust the springs accordingly.

Another tip for layout builders is to remove the screws that go up through the base and hold the cover in place before installing 022s on a permanent layout. That way you can perform routine maintenance without having to tear up long sections of track.

Final Checklist

If the switch motor is working, check the rail connections in the switch base. Examine the con-necting straps to see that they are properly soldered to the two control rails. This is a particularly common problem, because the solder lets go after a while. If you need to resolder them, use a good, hot iron and rosin-core solder. Never use acid-core solder for electrical work (fig. 5).

If the control rails are shorted against the ground or running rails, the switch will chatter continuously when the power is on. Tighten the center rail strap screw and also check for loose riveting that might result in faulty electrical contact.

When reassembling the switch, don't neglect to put the insulating paper between the switch base and its bottom plate. Bend up the soldered ends of the switch to make sure they make good contact with the connecting strap pins projecting from the switch base.

Then bend out the ground link connecting the outside rails so that it makes good contact with the switch motor frame. And finally, before you tighten the screws holding the switch motor to the base, make sure that the swivel rail pin is riding securely in its slot.

There! You have just repaired a wonderfully complex, antique, electromechanical combination relay/electrical switch/guidance/voltage supply device (otherwise known as the Lionel 022)! That wasn't so hard, was it?

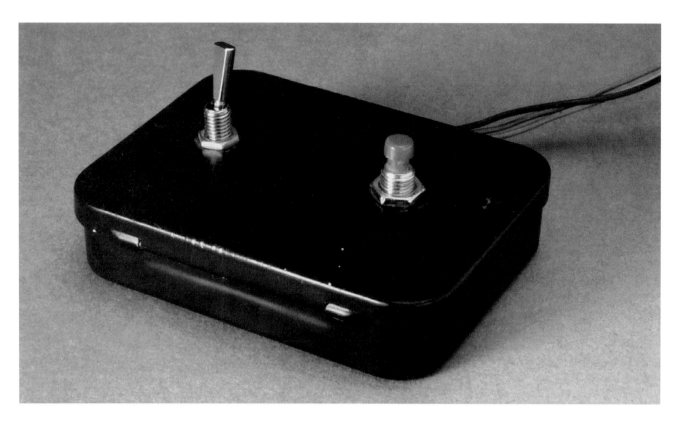

Too often you can buy terrific Lionel accessories *without* their controller. Don't despair; you can make your own!

PROJECT 6

Basic Accessory Controllers

So you bought a Lionel no. 97 coal elevator for a bargain price at a local swap meet. Then you discovered why it was so cheap—it didn't have a controller! You learned Plummer's First Law the hard way: "There are a lot more used accessories available than there are controllers."

Why is this? Original controllers are small and were easily lost. Many have Bakelite cases, which often crack or shatter upon even moderate impact. And I've long suspected that people who don't have adequate train display space must be collecting them.

When you looked for a replacement controller, you found that nobody was making them. The only solution was to find a used one somewhere. Then the only controllers you could find were either attached to other accessories or at the table of Rip Van Gouge, the not-too-friendly used parts dealer. And he wanted as much for the controller as you paid for the accessory!

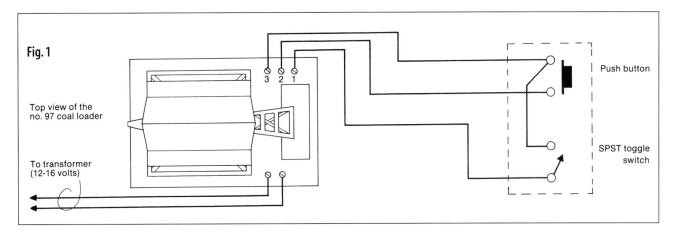

Fig. 1

Top view of the no. 97 coal loader

To transformer (12-16 volts)

3 2 1

Push button

SPST toggle switch

But there is a way out of this dilemma. Those modernistic-looking little black boxes that came with accessories contained nothing mysterious. Most housed simple on-off switches or push buttons. Replacements can be improvised with a minimum of skill, using parts from the neighborhood Radio Shack.

Types of Controllers

The Lionel postwar accessories that are listed in table 1 need only a basic push button to complete their electrical circuits and make them operate. Almost any kind of push-button switch can be used. Nine other Lionel accessories (listed in table 2) were packed with a common SPST (single-pole single-throw) on-off switch. Again, any kind of on-off switch can be used.

The no. 148 dwarf signal is also just one switch, but it is an SPDT

Fig. 2. (Below and right) The "experimenter box" version is sturdy and professional-looking.

Table 1. Push-button accessories

Number	Accessory
30	Water tower
114	Newsstand with horn
118	Newsstand with whistle
125	Whistling station
138	Water tower
161	Mail bag pickup
257	Freight station with horn
313	Bascule bridge
334	Dispatching board
415	Fueling station

Use Radio Shack 275-1566 or 275-1547B push buttons.

Table 2. SPST accessories

Number	Accessory
128	Animated newsstand
264	Fork lift platform
342	Culvert pipe loader
345	Culvert pipe unloader
356	Operating freight station
362	Operating barrel loader
364	Lumber loader
397	Coal loader
464	Lumber mill

Use Radio Shack 275-324 or 275-634 on-off switches.

(single-pole double-throw). This simply means it doesn't turn on and off. Instead, it routes the electricity to either the green or the red bulb, depending on which way it is thrown.

Building Time

Let's build a controller. We'll do one for the no. 97 coal elevator or no. 164 lumber loader. It has both a push button and an SPST switch. Figure 1 shows how the components are hooked up within the controller and how the three lead wires are connected to the numbered binding posts on the accessory.

If your layout has a control panel, the controller can be built

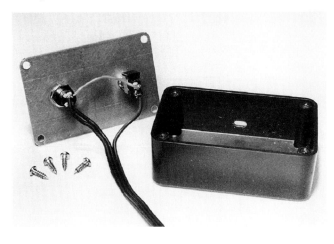

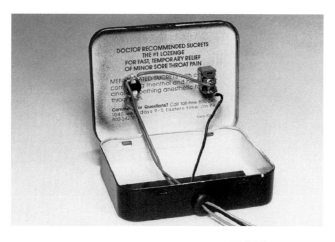
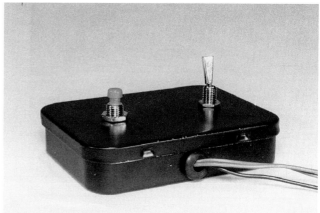

Fig. 3. (Above and above right) The author's "budget box" (an empty throat lozenges box) is as functional as the other controller, but a lot cheaper.

right in. If not, it can be housed in a number of ways. Any small metal or plastic box will do. If you're good with sheet metal, you can bend your own. "Experimenter boxes" from Radio Shack, designed to hold small components, come in various shapes and sizes. I used no. 270-230, which gives you plenty of working room.

My own favorite is the Sucrets throat lozenges box. Dump out the lozenges and save them for your next sore throat. Spray the box with satin black enamel, and you've got a first-class controller box, close to the original's dimensions.

In fact, I've built the controller with both kinds of boxes. The deluxe model in the experimenter box uses Radio Shack's nos. 275-1566 push button and 275-324 toggle switch. Three-conductor flat cable leads connect it to the accessory. See fig. 2.

The economy model in the Sucrets box uses the cheaper nos. 275-1547B button and 275-634 switch (fig. 3). Common 22-gauge stranded wire replaces the three-conductor flat cable. Because these boxes are shallow, line the

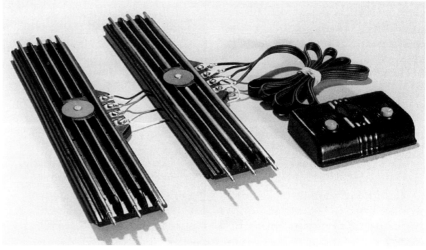

Fig. 4. Wiring UCS or RCS sections together provides an affordable alternative to purchasing and wiring separate controllers.

bottom with electrical tape to prevent accidental short circuits.

RCS and UCS Controllers

Most often missing are the controllers for Lionel remote-control and uncoupling track sections (RCS and UCS nos. 1019 and 6019). The two-button wafer-type arrangement Lionel devised for separate uncoupling and unloading functions requires sophisticated circuitry and push buttons to duplicate. These are more specialized and thus more expensive. Buying a new controller or a used one in good condition would probably

cost less than building your own.

If you're on a very tight budget, you can do what old Ray did back in his "shoestring and Sucrets box days." I parallel-wired remote-control sections together, using one controller to activate two or three tracks at the same time (fig. 4).

It works great, and since the only track that "works" is the one with a train on it, multiple operation makes little difference. Operation was a lot easier back then. Today I have a neatly symmetrical layout, with a separate controller for each section, and I keep hitting the wrong buttons.

The replacement controller for use with both the nos. 165 and 182 magnet cranes.

PROJECT 7

More-Complex Accessory Controllers

In the previous chapter, I described some basic techniques for building some of the more-common simple controllers. Now let's take on a few projects that are a little more complex—the no. 456 coal ramp, no. 497 coaling station, and the no. 165/182 magnet cranes. These accessories all had multi-function controllers that were specifically designed for them. Serviceable replacements can be fabricated with parts that are readily available from your local Radio Shack or other electronics supply store.

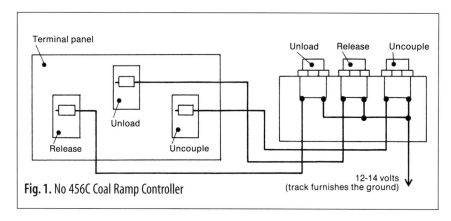

Fig. 1. No 456C Coal Ramp Controller

Labels in figure: Terminal panel, Unload, Release, Uncouple, Unload, Release, Uncouple, 12-14 volts (track furnishes the ground)

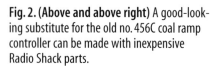

Fig. 2. (Above and above right) A good-looking substitute for the old no. 456C coal ramp controller can be made with inexpensive Radio Shack parts.

456 Coal Ramp

This popular item needs three push buttons to control the "uncouple," "unload," and "release" functions. Here's how the accessory works. A switch engine pushes the special hopper car to the top of the ramp. The hopper is locked into position by an electromagnetic knuckle coupler that's located inside the bumper at the end of the ramp. A touch of the "uncouple" button activates an electromagnet between the rails,

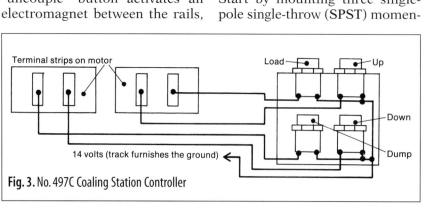

Fig. 3. No. 497C Coaling Station Controller

Labels in figure: Terminal strips on motor, Load, Up, Down, Dump, 14 volts (track furnishes the ground)

disengaging the hopper from the locomotive so the switcher can back down the ramp.

The car may then be unloaded at the operator's convenience by pushing the "unload" button. Another electromagnet between the rails opens the hopper doors, emptying the coal from the car. The third button, marked "release," opens the locking coupler and turns on the red light inside the head end of the ramp. The car rolls down the incline and is towed away by the waiting switcher.

Building the no. 456C controller is a straightforward job. Start by mounting three single-pole single-throw (SPST) momen-

tary contact push-button switches in a row. Each switch has two terminals. Wire all three switches together using one terminal on each. Run wire from the remaining terminals to the three posts on the coal ramp. Connect a single lead from the three interconnected terminals to a fixed voltage post on your transformer (I recommend 12 to 14 volts). The track acts as the ground connection for all circuits. See fig. 1.

I use Radio Shack no. 275-1566 push buttons. I mounted mine in a Radio Shack no. 270-230 experimenter box. It has plenty of room (fig. 2).

497 Coaling Station

This fascinating accessory has four basic actions. First, coal unloads from a dump car into the receiving bin, which is elevated to the top of the structure and emptied into a large hopper. Then the receiving bin lowers to track level. Throw the final switch, and the coal in the hopper is deposited into an empty car on the track below.

The four functions require only simple SPST momentary contact switches or push buttons

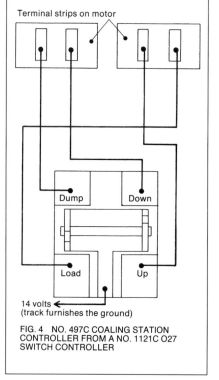

Labels in figure: Terminal strips on motor, Dump, Down, Load, Up, 14 volts (track furnishes the ground)

FIG. 4   NO. 497C COALING STATION CONTROLLER FROM A NO. 1121C O27 SWITCH CONTROLLER

Fig. 5. There are plenty of old no. 1121C O-27 switch controllers around, and they're easily converted for accessory operation. Remove the light bulb, and solder leads to both switch sides and the vacated bulb location.

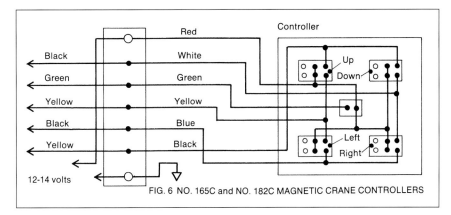

FIG. 6 NO. 165C and NO. 182C MAGNETIC CRANE CONTROLLERS

(fig. 3). A replacement controller can be fabricated using the same kind of push buttons and experimenter box as we used for the coal ramp. See fig. 2.

There is one difference: The original controller had levers instead of buttons or switches. If you prefer lever operation, you can construct a dual-lever controller from a discarded no. 1121C O-27 switch controller (fig. 4). It's easy to rewire, and it duplicates the action of the original.

To modify the no. 1121C, remove the old wiring and snip off the light socket with wire cutters. Connect your 14-volt power lead where the socket used to be, and solder the leads from the terminal strip on the accessory motor to the four contact lugs on the controller (fig. 5).

Because the levers are pivoted in the middle, the correct contact points used in each instance are opposite to the throw of the lever.

165 and 182 Magnet Cranes

Unlike most other accessories that clank and whir once they've been set into motion, the magnetic cranes are operator-intensive and require some skill. They are undoubtedly the most fascinating and busy accessories that the Lionel Corp. ever devised.

Five basic controls energize the magnet, raise or lower the cable, and rotate the cab/boom assembly left or right in a complete circle. A hand wheel at the rear of the cab controls the position of the boom itself.

The original no. 165C controller is used for both cranes. It contains four of Lionel's famous wafer-switch push buttons and a rotary "on-off" switch.

The buttons on the right side control the vertical action of the cable. The left-hand buttons control the horizontal action of the cab/boom assembly. The rotary switch in the center energizes the magnet and the red light inside the cab. All the no. 165C's functions can be duplicated using four double-pole double-throw (DPDT) momentary contact push buttons and a simple SPST toggle switch. See fig. 6.

Note that only one terminal of each DPDT switch is used in this design. But there's a catch. You must use the terminal side where the normally open contacts are closed when the button is pushed. To determine the correct side, use a continuity tester from a hardware store or just low-voltage current and a light bulb.

The center poles have to be connected together. I use four Alcoswitch no. MPA-206R miniature push buttons and a Radio Shack no. 275-324 toggle in a Radio Shack no. 270-231 experimenter box. The wiring is consistently color-coded for clarity. See photo of finished controller on page 31.

Lionel promoted "remote control" as a high-tech aspect of its trains. Operating knuckle couplers were the most common of the remote-control features Lionel offered.

PROJECT 8

Knuckle Couplers

More than a half century ago, Lionel introduced the "Real Railroad Knuckle Coupler." It was a quantum leap toward more realistic toy trains. Although there have been a number of engineering changes over the years, the basic concept and design remain, making the knuckle coupler one of the longest-running and most reliable Lionel inventions. The knuckle became standard on all O gauge rolling stock, regardless of size or relative proportion. From that day forward, any Lionel locomotive or car could be used in conjunction with any other.

The quickest way to fix a broken coupler is to replace the whole thing. Where there is severe damage, that might be prudent, but usually with a little effort (and a lot less money) the old one can be satisfactorily repaired. Often, cleaning, lubrication, and simple adjustments or replacing minor parts will be all that's needed. Most parts are available from Lionel parts dealers.

Major Knuckle Coupler Components

• **The knuckle itself.** Made of die-cast metal or of Delrin (a special low-friction plastic), the knuckle usually pivots on a long rivet. It is spring-loaded, and when properly adjusted, will pop open smartly when released.

• **The coupler head (or knuckle housing).** This holds the knuckle in place. It is hollow, providing space for the locking cam behind the knuckle to move. Whether it is made of metal, styrene plastic, or Delrin, its basic shape hasn't changed much over the years.

• **The activator (or release) mechanism.** There have been many variations on this, so let's take the main ones chronologically:

Known as the "coil coupler," Lionel's earliest knuckle coupler was made from 1945 to 1949. It was an outgrowth of the prewar box-coupler mechanism, which used a cumbersome solenoid-and-plunger device to lift the boxes. Power for the coil is picked up through a slider shoe from a special five-rail track section. The knuckle is kept in place by pressure from a small spring-loaded plunger within the solenoid coil. When current is applied, the plunger is pulled back, releasing the locking cam on the knuckle and allowing the coupler to spring open.

Next came the magnetic coupler, first appearing in Lionel's 1948 line. By the next year, most Lionel rolling stock had been converted to it. Instead of having an electromagnetic coil on each truck, one coil was placed in a special track section. This was the

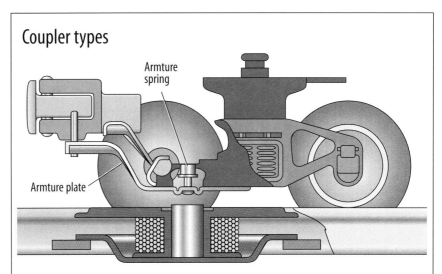

Positioned over an uncoupling track, the magnetic coupler's knuckle snaps open when the movable armature plate on the truck bottom is attracted by the energized electromagnet.

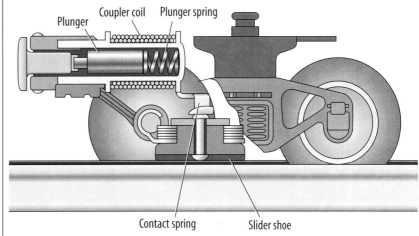

The coil coupler's knuckle snaps open when the coupler coil is energized through the coupler's truck slider shoe as it contacts an energized control rail on an uncoupler track.

first version of the basic uncoupling principle still in use today. The locking cam on the knuckle is kept in place by a pin on the end of a spring-loaded armature plate.

When energized, the track magnet pulls the armature plate down, and the knuckle is released.

The disc coupler, which came out in 1957, is part of a one-piece molded styrene plastic unit that includes the coupler head, arm, truck bolster and side frames. The activating armature is a narrow spring-steel strip with a pin on one end and a metal disc hanging from a round shank in the middle of it. It functions in the same way

The foundation of train operations: the knuckle coupler. You can clearly see the knuckle, knuckle head, and the activator of the disc coupler.

It's easy to track the evolution of the knuckle coupler. From left to right are the coil coupler, the magnetic coupler, disc coupler, and MPC-and-later disc coupler.

The coupler disassembled. Next to the detached coupler head and rivet, you can clearly see the cast-on lug that holds the coupler to the coupler arm.

as the previous magnetic coupler.

The 1970s Lionel/MPC version of the disc coupler works on the same principle, but was redesigned to make use of different materials. A snap-in Delrin armature, with pin and shank molded on, replaced the metal parts. To make the couplers operate over the track magnet, Lionel engineers came up with an ingenious device—something like an ordinary large thumbtack, inserted into the hollow shank.

These are the four basic activating mechanisms, although there have been many sub-variations within each. The one currently being produced by Lionel LLC is essentially the same as the Lionel/MPC device of the 1970s.

Coupler Troubleshooting

• **Loose coupler head.** This problem is often encountered with the die-cast metal models. It can hamper coupler function and, if it is not fixed, the coupler's head will eventually come off.

The coupler head is held in place by a cast-on lug (or nipple) that fits through a hole in the sheet-metal coupler arm. During coupler assembly, the lug is peened over. Usually a few taps with a punch or ball peen hammer will secure it again. Don't pound too hard or you might distort the hollow coupler head and ruin it.

If the nipple is broken off, the head can be bonded back in place

with epoxy or a gel-type cement. This repair won't work with coil couplers, because the glue layer will act as an insulator and disrupt the electrical circuit.

There are many reasons that a coupler won't open.

• **Broken knuckle spring.** This is a fairly common malady that

Below. Use a punch and hammer to secure the rivets.

Right. The components of a coil coupler: the slider shoe assembly, the fiberboard strip, the coil coupler assembly, and the rivet.

Below right. To remove a rivet, file off the rivet head.

isn't really critical. When activated, the weight of the train pulling against the knuckle will force it open. However, if you are fussy and want your knuckles to pop open smartly, the springs can be replaced. After you've replaced a few of these, however, you might not be so fussy!

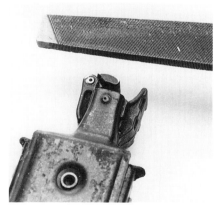

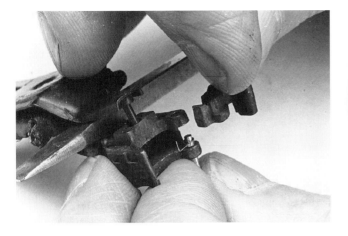

You may need to use a screwdriver to wedge the armature plate of a magnetic coupler up in order to install a coupler head and spring.

Take care in riveting the fiberboard strip into place on a coil coupler.

Most couplers, except those made for a time during the 1960s, use a coil spring wrapped around the rivet that holds the knuckle in place. The repair procedure is the same for all of them.

First, invert the truck. You should then file off the flared end of the rivet and pull it out. Discard the old rivet and the broken spring.

During the next step the activator pin must be kept out of the way. With recent Lionel/MPC or LTI products, simply remove the Delrin armature. For the older models, wedge a screwdriver between the armature plate or spring and the coupler arm.

Thread the new rivet through the coupler hole. Insert the new spring exactly as shown. Reinstall the knuckle and push the rivet through the second hole. Using a rivet punch, flare the end of the rivet just enough so it stays in place. Too much flaring can cause the knuckle to bind. Test the action. The knuckle should pop open. If it doesn't, remove the rivet and try again. You'll soon get the hang of it.

Those one-piece Delrin knuckles of the 1960s are another matter. As a cost-cutting measure, a flat spring and two pivot points were molded right onto the knuckle. This design was scrapped after a few years because they were so fragile. Replacement knuckles have the plastic springs attached to them, but are installed with rivets.

• **Faulty activator mechanism (coil couplers).** The coil couplers are the most troublesome because of their complexity, since they have both electrical and mechanical components.

The most common problem is dirty contacts. Clean both ends of the slider shoe rivet with mineral spirits. Make sure that the leaf-spring contact on the inside is pressing firmly against the shoe rivet. If these surfaces are oxidized or corroded, dress them lightly with a fine file or emery board.

Check the fine wire leading from the coil to the leaf spring. It should be soldered to the lug on the fiberboard terminal strip behind the coil. If the wire is broken, it may be necessary to carefully unwind one turn of the coil and then reattach it. Remember, this wire is coated with an enamel that must be removed before it can be soldered. Very fine sandpaper works best.

If the slider shoe assembly is broken or missing, it should be replaced. New shoes, rivets, and fiber retaining plates are available. Assemble the shoe with its straight edge facing the outside of the truck. Bend the contact spring out of the way if necessary. Rest the rivet head solidly on a metal block and flare it with a rivet punch. Bend the contact spring back into place. Be sure that the new shoe doesn't bind and that there is adequate spring tension before you reassemble the truck.

Sometimes the plunger may stick, which keeps the knuckle from opening (or closing) properly. A few squirts of WD-40 into the coupler head will usually dissolve the gunk and free up the action. A sticking plunger could also indicate a warped or damaged solenoid tube, caused by overheating or mishandling. In that fairly rare instance, I recommend replacement of the entire unit.

• **Faulty activator mechanism (magnetic couplers).** A magnetic coupler knuckle that fails to open is usually a symptom of poor alignment of the armature pin within the coupler head. Check manually to see that the armature plate works freely. Adjust the bend in its neck with pliers until it does. The pin should always be vertical and move easily in and out of the hole in the head of the coupler.

It is also possible that the armature leaf spring is exerting too much pressure for the track magnet to work it effectively. Gently bend the spring on both sides of the rivet until the excess pressure is relieved.

The armature plate may be too far above the track magnet. It can be bent slightly to bring it closer to the track. Disc couplers are rarely subject to this kind of malady if the leaf-spring armature hasn't been mangled in some way. If it has, try to bend it straight.

Occasionally, the cylindrical

Remember to rebend the contact spring into place when reassembling coil couplers.

By slightly bending the neck of the armature plate of a coil coupler, you may be able to improve activator performance.

Adjusting the armature leaf spring and releasing some of the tension may also improve the activator function.

shank from which the disc is suspended will hang up on the coupler arm or on some part of the car underbody. This most often happens when the car has been tipped upside down before being put on the rails. Remedies must be handled on a case-by-case basis.

You should know that the knuckle on the post-1970 MPC/LTI couplers might not open if the snap-in Delrin armature isn't snapped in all the way or if the thumbtack has fallen out of its hole in the coupler shank.

• **Knuckle won't stay closed (coil coupler).** With a coil coupler, this usually indicates a broken or weakened plunger spring. These springs collapse if overheated repeatedly and they should be replaced. It could also be caused by a sticking plunger, so spray WD-40 into it before you take it apart.

The Lionel service manual recommends forcing the knuckle open with diagonal cutting pliers to get at the spring and plunger. I've had rather bad luck with that because some of the knuckles have become brittle with age. Usually I just remove and replace the rivet when changing plunger springs, installing a new knuckle spring at the same time.

• **Knuckle won't stay closed (magnetic coupler).** The two main causes of this kind of knuckle failure with the metal magnetic couplers are a loose coupler head or not enough tension on the flat armature spring. Both coupler problems can be remedied easily.

The die-cast nipple is inaccessible with the armature plate in place, so if you wanted to re-peen it, it would require removing the whole plate assembly. The simplest way to deal with a loose head is by putting a dab of epoxy cement under it.

Tension can also be increased by riveting the spring a little more tightly or by gently bending it with narrow-nose pliers. Be careful because the springs can break, particularly if creased from previous adjustments.

Disc couplers that act up in this way can be difficult to repair. When the knuckle won't stay closed, it usually means that the flat-spring armature pin assembly has been bent, warped, twisted, or weakened in some way. This should be obvious by looking at it. If you're lucky, you might be able to bend it back the way it was.

Because the armature spring is tightly riveted to the coupler arm, itself an integral part of the molded truck, which is in turn usually riveted to the car body, getting at the rivet to replace it can be very difficult. This is an instance where truck replacement is strongly indicated.

If the car has a metal floor, heat the bolster rivet with a soldering iron until the plastic truck melts and comes off. Saw the rivet in half and start over with a different truck and a new rivet. If the car body is plastic, you have my deepest sympathy. There is no way to get the truck off without trashing

the car in the process. I would suggest that you either make a fixed coupler out of it by gluing the knuckle in place or contribute the car to your neighborhood plastic recycling program.

The post-1970 MPC/LTI cars with this problem can usually be fixed by replacing the snap-in Delrin armatures. Sometimes the armatures can be bent back to their original shape, seating them firmly and flatly against the coupler arm. This works for a while if the little pins are still in good shape. Because some of these armatures are apparently stronger than others, experimentation is in order. Keep changing armatures until you find one that will do the job to your satisfaction.

There comes a point, however, where the weight of the train is just too great for any armature to hold itself in position and the knuckle springs open. Today's powerful locomotives and needle-bearing trucks permit running trains longer than ever before, but the coupler technology has not kept up.

I know an operator who wraps twist-ties from his wife's freezer bags around his coupler arms to keep the armatures from popping out. It works for him.

The next time half of your train goes wooshing by, while the other half remains in the tunnel, you'll know what to do once you get the train stopped, because now you know all the secrets of the art of coupler repair!

Repairing Lionel's
Operating Cars and Accessories

For 30 years, Lionel cars were not expected to do anything but look good in the trains. Sure, some of the better passenger cars had interior lights, but that was it. At the beginning of the 1930s, manually operated crane and floodlight cars were tentatively introduced. By the end of the decade, cars were automatically dumping coal, unloading logs and throwing off barrels and packing cases.

During the postwar era, the operating car came into its own. Lionel's development engineers outdid themselves attempting to produce model freight cars that imitated every function of the real ones, such as moving horses and cows onto the train, and a good many that prototype cars were not expected to do, like launching aircraft, firing missiles, and exploding upon impact.

In this section, we will deal with three such car types, encompassing most of the postwar era, and covering all of the basic action mechanisms Lionel used on these cars—springs, mechanical linkages, solenoids, and vibration motors and combinations thereof.

Lionel has made trackside accessories to go with their electric trains almost from the beginning. The early ones were mainly decorative and passive, designed to add railroad atmosphere to the toy train layout—tunnels, bridges, stations, and signals. By the 1920s, a few provided illumination, but not much else.

From the mid-1930s on through the 1950s, the Lionel engineering department, in a series of bursts of creative imagination, began designing accessories that actually did something—providing a new dimension of action to augment the sights and sounds of trains running around the track, and enhancing the illusion of the real world in miniature. Suddenly, the toy train layout was lifted to another level of enjoyment and fun.

It is our job in this section to keep those operating accessories pumping. We've chosen a cross-section of popular accessories, as well as a couple of less common ones that were delightfully sophisticated in their engineering, and the toy train wonders of their age.

The Automatic Gateman

Without question, the most popular Lionel accessory of all time was the automatic gateman. For over 60 years, he faithfully came out of his shanty, waving a red lantern to warn motorists of the approaching train. Almost all of the other train manufacturers all over the world produced their own versions of the gateman accessory—even the Russians had one that looked suspiciously like a direct copy of the Lionel piece.

Coal Accessories

Hauling coal was a major occupation on the Lionel Lines in the 1940s and '50s, mirroring the importance of the "black diamonds" to American society at the time. Lionel made coal accessories that totally captured the imagination. They all were great fun to operate or just to watch in action. They probably spilled more coal than they loaded.

Lumber Accessories

Second only to coal in Lionelville was the logging industry. As with coal, there were two appropriate accessories—one with an endless chain and the other with a conveyor belt to move the dowel "logs" from car to car.

Lionel Magnet Cranes

Electromagnetic cranes were the most entertaining accessories that Lionel produced. Mechanically sophisticated and versatile, the cranes required more operator skill and coordination than the other accessories. It took time to learn how to use the crane to load and unload pieces of scrap steel successfully.

The Transfer Table

This accessory, which paid homage to the advent of dieselization on the Lionel Lines, also extracted a fair amount of acquired operator skill to align the rails correctly. Many a Geep and F3 wound up with its flanges in the dirt before the table jockey learned his craft. Running the transfer table successfully (even most of the time) inspired a great sense of operator accomplishment.

The Operating Freight Station

Adding a dimension of mayhem and frenzy to the tranquil Lionelville scene, the operating freight station featured two baggage cart drivers who automatically sped in and out of the station, propelling their vehicles on what amounted to an oval race track. This one often made spectators dizzy.

The Bascule Bridge

The engineering department's magnum opus accessory was undoubtedly the bascule bridge. It provided a new dimension of danger for the trains on the layout, and another variable impediment to keeping the *Lionel Limited* running on time. A real crowd-pleaser.

The Lionel Corp.'s massive no. 456 operating coal ramp, with its no. 3456 Norfolk & Western operating hopper, introduced mining operations to many children in the early 1950s. Fixing an original 456 isn't difficult if you know what to do.

PROJECT 9

Coal Ramp Set No. 456

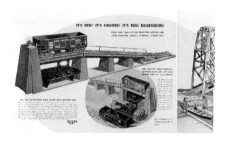

This illustration from the 1950 consumer catalog shows how the ramp could be combined with the no. 397 operating coal loader. As coal fell into the ramp's bin, the coal loader scooped it up and dumped it into a hopper that was waiting on an adjacent siding.

Some people say bigger is better. Perhaps the Lionel Corp. thought so too when, from 1950 to 1955, it marketed a coal ramp accessory that was three feet long. Just as children were enthralled by the gargantuan no. 456 ramp more than 40 years ago, collectors and operators today love to watch its special hopper car empty its load.

But not all coal ramps can dump with the best of them anymore. Problems with the hopper doors, electromagnetic couplers, ramp rails, and controller, as well as other features, are common. But with a little improvising, it's easy to revamp the coal ramp and get it moving loads of black diamonds in short order.

The doors on the bottom of the operating hopper sometimes don't open properly. Use pliers to slightly bend the metal fingers on either side of the round plunging plate assembly to alleviate any potential problems with the unloading of coal.

How It Worked

In its heyday, the no. 456 operating coal ramp was a natural for the end of a siding in an industrial area and a simple accessory that worked extremely well. But because of its length, it required more space than most small or even medium-sized layouts could spare.

The ramp came with a three-button controller, a bag of artificial coal, and a special no. 3456 Norfolk & Western operating hopper car. The action sequence began after the loaded hopper was pushed up the ramp by a locomotive and a short consist of "idler" cars. At the top, a knuckle coupler concealed in the end pier locked the hopper into position.

Then, touching the three buttons on the controller brought the ramp to life. The "uncouple" button energized an electromagnet at the other end of the hopper, separating it from the rest of the consist and locomotive, which could all be backed down and out of the way.

The "unload" button energized a second electromagnet underneath the hopper that pulled its bottom doors open and allowed the coal to drain out between the rails and into the bin under the ramp. The natural vibration of the electromagnet shook the car enough so that most of the coal actually dropped through.

The "release" button opened the coupler knuckle in the end pier, freeing the empty hopper from its perch. A big red light atop the pier flashed, warning all concerned that the car was loose and rolling down the ramp. The sequence ended as the switch engine once again towed away the empty hopper.

Lionel catalogs almost always showed the ramp working alongside the no. 397 operating diesel-type coal loader. Children could use a bridge pin to place a plastic bin (no. 456-83) between the two accessories for continuous activity. After the coal flowed into the bin beneath the rails, the conveyor belt on the loader lifted it into an empty hopper that was waiting on an adjoining siding.

The action of the ramp was nearly foolproof because the ramp relied mainly on gravity. There were no real moving parts and few critical adjustments, which is why most no. 456 coal ramps found today can be returned to working order quite easily.

Common Problems

The ramps themselves were ruggedly constructed, but several common weaknesses in the mechanisms often show up.

First, after repeated use, the dumping doors on the hopper sometimes become so loose that they no longer retain the coal load. Without this function, the coal ramp loses nearly all of its effectiveness.

Bending the fingers on the plunging plate assembly with a small pair of pliers will tighten the doors and increase the tension when they close. But do this carefully. A little bending goes a long way.

If, however, the doors aren't just loose but broken, they should be replaced. Lionel parts dealers often have them in stock or can order them for you.

If the electromagnetic knuckle coupler built into the head of the ramp no longer functions, you should replace it with an original Lionel part. A coupler-coil assembly from an old freight car truck can also be used, but it won't work as smoothly as the original, which had a special "easy-locking" knuckle (no. 456-25) in it.

If you can, remove the special knuckle from the original and mount it in the replacement assembly. The correct rivets (no. TC-23) and springs (no. TC-22) are available from most Lionel parts suppliers.

Fortunately for the Lionel enthusiast, the electromagnets between the rails that dump the hopper's load are sturdy and well-protected. Unless the accessory was stored upside down on a wet basement floor for years, these two electromagnets should work. If they don't, only original parts (no. 456-54) can replace them.

Sometimes the two aluminum extrusions that form the ramp rails are bent because of mishandling or improper storage. With the pliers, do a little "body and fender" work on them, making them as straight as possible. There should be no kinks or narrow spots in the track gauge that could impede the empty car's smooth roll down the ramp.

Name and Number: Operating coal ramp no. 456 and operating hopper car

General maintenance: Very little is required. Keep ramp clean and axles oiled.

Maintenance schedule: As needed.

Troubleshooting:

1. Loose hopper doors—Tighten by bending "fingers" on plunger plate to increase tension.

2. Car doesn't roll freely—Oil car axles. Check for binding in trucks. Shim head end of ramp slightly

3. Electromagnets between rails or in built-in head coupler not functioning—Check for broken wires or bad insulation, usually in cable connecting controller with accessory.

Because the ramp operates on fixed voltage grounded through the running rails, it's also important the ramp rails be firmly attached to the ramp base with a pair of roundhead screws. Use no. 4-40 x ³⁄₁₆″ screws for O gauge, no. 2-56 x ³⁄₁₆″ screws for O-27 gauge.

The heart of the accessory's action, the controller, can be another source of problems. It contains three simple push-button switches. But the wiring occasionally can fray or burn out, perhaps from hours of young hands pressing the buttons. A substitute can be fabricated with parts from Radio Shack. See Chapters 6 and 7.

The flexible "handrail" that parallels the rails from the foot to the head of the ramp is often broken or missing. On the early, dark gray variations of the ramp, Lionel used a special fabric-covered braided wire for the handrail. For later, light gray versions, the company used fishing line. So feel free to use heavy black fishing line as a substitute. Be sure to pull it tight when threading it through the handrail postholes.

While nearly all of these fixes may seem minor, each in one way or another significantly affects how smoothly the ramp mechanisms move.

Bringing the Ramp Up to Speed

Beyond repair of the common problems, several modifications to the ramp can also improve its performance. Although Lionel didn't have the foresight to include these features when the ramp was first designed, they'll certainly help make its operation better.

If the ramp doesn't have enough slant for the hopper to roll down once it's emptied itself, heighten it by inserting a small shim or spacer under the ramp's bumper end to increase the grade slightly. Of course, keeping the hopper's wheels lubricated helps it roll better too.

Another improvement several operators have tried is substituting one of the nos. 6105 Reading, 6109 Chesapeake & Ohio, or 6117 Erie operating hopper cars that Model Products Corp./Fundimensions manufactured in the early 1980s for the 3456 hopper that comes with the ramp. These cars can be made to work by moving the uncoupling magnet between the rails slightly to match their longer coupler shanks.

A few hours with these repairs and your coal ramp can once again bring hours of entertainment, ensuring that your layout's miners won't be laid off and living on toy train pension funds.

PROJECT 10
Coal Loader No. 397

L ionel's entertaining no. 397 diesel-type operating coal loader was patterned after a common piece of trackside equipment used by the coal industry and railroads. Motor-driven, conveyor-belt loaders vaguely resembling Lionel's have long been used at locations too small to warrant heavy coal-handling facilities.

The Lionel loader, cataloged from 1948 through 1957, has a gray die-cast base, a red plastic scoop-like holding bin or tray, and either a yellow or blue simulated General Motors stationary diesel engine. The "engine" is actually a hollow plastic shell that conceals a real electric motor. Early runs of the no. 397 were illuminated by a small no. 70 yard light attached to a pole at the rear corner of the base.

Old no. 397 rocks and rolls and throws coal all over the layout—and that's a lot of the fun of this accessory, illustrated in the 1949 catalog (above).

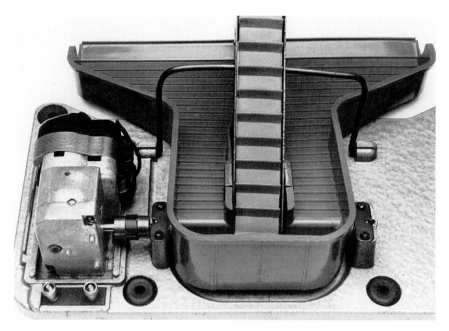

Fig. 1. The first steps in replacing a worn-out belt are to remove the heavy-wire supports and the two shaft-bearing cover plates toward the rear of the base.

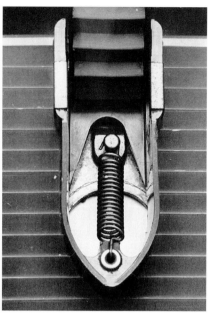

Fig. 2. Remove the scoop by releasing the spring beneath the conveyor assembly.

Loading and Unloading

In operation, coal unloaded into the holding tray can later be reloaded into another railroad car at the same track location—not very satisfying for those who prefer realistic operation. A continuous cycle of dumping and loading could be set up using the 397 in conjunction with the no. 456 coal ramp. A special bin packed with the ramp fits on the coal loader.

When the 397 is activated, the pile of coal at the front of the holding tray is agitated by a sharp reciprocating motion in the tray, causing the coal to work its way up into a bin at the rear of the accessory. There it's picked up by the conveyor belt, lifted to an appropriate height, and deposited into a waiting empty car. The coal shakes, rattles, and spills as it moves up the conveyor. Some of it actually reaches the car.

Baling Wire and Chewing Gum

A recurring problem is with stray coal lumps that get caught under the conveyor belt, jamming up the works. This was particularly troublesome on the early models. Lionel redesigned the conveyor beam and added cover clips as a remedy, but the fix wasn't per-fect. The loaders still jammed, only not as often. So, be prepared to poke out the coal pieces that occasionally get stuck under the belt. It's all part of the fun.

To further minimize the problem, the factory service manual recommended using only genuine Lionel no. 206 artificial coal, because it had been screened to a uniform size. (So far, so credible.) But then it went on to recommend wrapping a strip of masking tape or Scotch Tape around the beam spacers. (How about baling wire and chewing gum?) If Lionel's engineers couldn't come up with a better solution in 10 years of production, I suppose we'll have to consider this a kind of genetic defect and live with it.

An almost universal problem, even with coal loaders that have never been used, is a deteriorated conveyor belt. After 35 or 40 years, the character of the rubber changes. Some belts become soft and tacky; others get dried out and crack or stretch. In either case, they don't work well any more.

Fortunately, excellent quality replacements are available, so plan on installing a new belt if you intend to operate your coal loader. If your unit is one of the later models with a black rubberized flexible drive coupling between the gearbox and main shaft, it's a good idea to replace that too, even if it still looks okay. (It's like having a 30-year-old tire on your truck—you never know when it will let go.)

Belt Removal

To replace the belt (fig. 1), you must separate the conveyor, tray assembly, and base from each other. Start by removing the plastic motor cover held in place by one thumb-screw.

Work the heavy-wire conveyor supports out of their moorings in the base by squeezing them together; they'll pop right out.

Next, remove the two shaft-bearing cover plates toward the rear of the base; they're held in place by two screws. After releasing the spring that holds the base and tray together (fig. 2), carefully lift the tray from the base, working the shaft coupling free of the drive coupling as you proceed.

With the tray on its side and the coupling end of the shaft down, remove the exposed square bronze bearing. See fig. 3. Gently tap the end of the shaft with a small hammer until the cam slides

Fig. 3. Care is required in removing the shaft from the tray. After removing the exposed square bronze bearing, gently tap on the end of the shaft with a small hammer.

Fig. 4. Disassembly is complete once you've removed the retaining washer from the end of the conveyor assembly. This releases the pin, idler roller, and separator-and-shield assembly.

Name and Number: Diesel-style operating coal loader no. 397
General maintenance: Lubricate gearbox with two drops of oil through motor cover screw hole. Lubricate shaft end bearings with one drop through openings. Apply sparingly. Motor needs occasional tune-up and/or cleaning. Keep areas around motor and exposed mechanism as free of dirt as possible.
Maintenance schedule: As needed.
Troubleshooting:
1. Motor doesn't run—Check for broken wires leading to it, also sticking brush or dirty commutator. Motors rarely burn out.
2. Motor runs slowly—Needs tune-up. Check for binds in the mechanism.
3. Motor runs; belt does not—Belt stretched or badly worn. Check drive coupling between gearbox and conveyor. Check for stray pieces of coal stuck under belt.
4. Coal collects on one side—Make sure that the cams are in identical position.

off and the beam assembly can be removed from the tray. Be very careful. If you hit it too hard, you may break the plastic tray. Try not to dislodge the other cam; that will allow you to use it as a guide during reassembly. (If the accessory has been stored in a damp environment, the cams may be rusted tight to the shaft. Soak them in penetrating oil until they free up.)

Now, remove the retaining washer (horseshoe clip) from the pin at the top end of the conveyor (fig. 4). Using a punch, drive the pin out. Before removing the old belt, note how it's positioned on the conveyor assembly with regard to the protruding "trays." The new belt must be put on the same way. If you put the belt on backwards, the coal will slide off before it reaches the top.

Belt Tightening

Install the new belt. Be prepared for a tough stretch. The belt has to be tight or it won't work. Be sure you put the idler roller in position between the beams before you begin.

Replace the pin through the separator-and-shield assembly, the conveyor beams, and the idler roller. Because of the tight fit, you may need an extra pair of hands for this operation.

Reattach the retaining washer, and the job is complete. Test the belt assembly by hand to be sure there's no binding. A little Teflon powder (or corn starch) applied to the inside of the belt at this point will smooth out the action.

Reassemble the accessory by retracing the steps you took during disassembly.

Make sure both cams are positioned on the square shaft in exactly the same way. They must pull the tray back in tandem with each other. If they don't, the action will be out of synchronization, and the accessory will do a dance that bears some resemblance to the samba.

Aside from the conveyor belt and drive coupling replacement, the no. 397 is fairly maintenance free. For optimum performance, it should be hooked directly to a separate fixed-voltage circuit and operated at 12 to 15 volts.

The heavy-duty motor requires occasional cleaning. (See Chapter 1.) The gearbox is very solid. It should be lubricated lightly (two drops of oil) through the motor cover screw hole, followed by a short squeeze of Lionel lubricant. The shaft bearings should also be oiled occasionally with a drop or two through the openings in their covers.

That's it. With a little lubrication, your coal loader will spray coal all over your layout for hour after hour!

PROJECT 11

Automatic Merchandise Car No. 3454

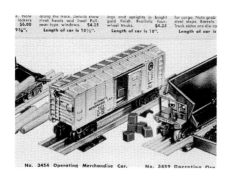

Lionel's no. 3454 automatic merchandise car, cataloged in 1946 and 1947 only, was upstaged by the popular milk car. Even so, it's still a crowd-pleaser in its own right.

Everyone who loves Lionel trains should have an automatic merchandise car. Lionel cataloged three different ones between 1939 and 1947, and each uses the same type of remote-control mechanism to supply lots of action and fun. In addition, these cars are easy to maintain and repair.

All three merchandise cars offer the kind of realistic yet fanciful action that makes toy trains such a delight. The idea behind them is to simulate packing cases being tossed from a boxcar, as would have been seen at any freight station of the period.

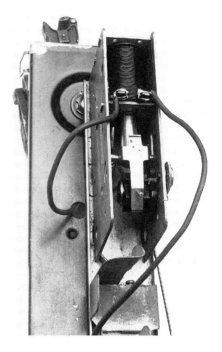

(Above) The top of the chute on the left is directly beneath the roof hatch. The ejection seat is in the center, and the operating mechanism is on the right. The arm and the wire attached to the mechanism open and close the door. The small hook at the end of the wire fits over a pin on the inside of the door.

(Above right) This closeup of the operating mechanism in the closed-door position shows the spring that causes the arm to snap back and close the door after unloading six packing crates. When the mechanism is in the open-door position, the arm is closer to the right.

(Right) This top view of the operating mechanism shows the solenoid, pawl, and ratchet. Note the similarity between this and Lionel's E-unit reversing mechanism.

Name and Number: Automatic merchandise car no. 3454
General maintenance: Little required. Keep car clean inside and out. Lubricate internal bearings and shafts sparingly. Do not oil solenoid.
Maintenance schedule: As needed.
Troubleshooting:
1. Mechanism does not operate—Check pickup shoes and wires running from them to solenoid for dirt, deterioration, and breakage. Repair or replace as necessary. Check continuity of solenoid coil.
2. Generally sluggish action—Increase voltage to track. Clean solenoid plunger. Check internal bearings and linkages for freedom from binding. Lubricate and/or adjust as needed.
3. Door action slow or incomplete—Check for bent or loose door guides. Clean door slots. Lubricate pivot bearing.
4. Boxes stick in chute—Polish chute with automotive chrome polish. Follow with furniture wax, if desired.

Action

All you need to start the action is a five-rail RCS or no. 1019 remote-control track. Load the crates through a hinged hatch in the roof; they stack up in a chute leading to an ejection seat that's part of the mechanism in the middle of the car. Next, press a button on the remote control to activate a spring-loaded solenoid. That triggers a bar linkage, which strikes the bottom of an ejection seat and forces it upward to toss out a plastic crate.

Lionel brought out its first O gauge merchandise car, no. 3814, in 1939 and cataloged it through 1942. This sheet-metal boxcar has an automatic mechanism mounted inside, along with a chute that can hold as many as 15 small plastic packing crates. (Postwar cars came with only six crates.)

At the same time, a pawl on the end of the plunger advances a six-tooth ratchet wheel one notch at a time. An indentation on the edge of the ratchet wheel controls the opening of the car door. The door is connected to a spring-loaded arm that keeps it closed after the mechanism goes through a complete cycle. Each time you press the unload button, another crate is ejected until the sixth one hits the cinders. Then the door automatically closes, even though the chute isn't empty.

After the war, Lionel cataloged two other merchandise cars (nos. 3454 and 3854) with an improved mechanism. Both were cataloged in 1946 and 1947 though the 9¼"-long no. 3454 is far more common.

Like the prewar 3814, the O-27 gauge 3454 works with either the five-rail RCS track of the later UCS and no. 6019 tracks. The longer 3854 isn't so accommodating. Because of its near-scale length, the 3854 can't fit both trucks on the UCS or 6019 remote-control tracks and so can't be operated with them. It requires the old RCS or 1019 tracks.

Service

The mechanism used on Lionel's merchandise cars is one of the simplest the firm ever made. The solenoid, ratchet, and pawl are similar to Lionel's E-unit for reversing locomotive direction. Still, you may find your merchandise car isn't operating as smoothly or reliably as you'd like. Here are some things you should watch for:

• Wires leading from the truck pickup shoes to the solenoid coil should be soldered firmly in place. Replace them if they've deteriorated with age.

• Contacts on the pickup shoes should be clean and shiny.

• Door must seat squarely and move freely in the guides. Remove any dirt or dust accumulation from the guide slots. Make sure the door doesn't bind due to bent or loose guides.

• Delivery chute inside the car should be as smooth as possible. Remove all roughness caused by dirt and oxidation with automotive chrome polish. Make it shine, then follow with furniture wax.

• Solenoid plunger must be clean and move in and out freely. Clean it with TV tuner cleaner or mineral spirits, then dry it with cotton swabs. Don't use lubricants.

• Apply one drop of oil to all bearing surfaces and shafts, but not the plunger.

Get One!

Lionel's merchandise car fits in anywhere on a layout. Logs, lumber, and barrels belong in industrial areas, but packing crates can be unloaded just about anywhere: passenger and freight stations, loading docks, and team tracks. Besides, like other Lionel operating cars, a merchandise car keeps visitors fascinated for a long time.

Be aware that whenever the car is unloading, the coupler knuckles on both ends open. This glitch is quite common to operating cars with coil couplers. Also, the coupler coils tend to heat up if the car is used without interruption. This can cause couplers to warp or burn out. If you plan to operate your merchandise car, you should consider replacing the original trucks with the later, magnetic kind.

This problem shouldn't have kept the popular 3454 from being cataloged after 1947. But that was the year Lionel introduced the no. 3462 operating milk car. Like the 3454, it unloaded freight that was hidden from view. But with a more familiar load and a moving human figure, 3462 surpassed whatever the merchandise car could offer. The milk car became a milestone in Lionel's history. Still, we should not forget its wonderful forerunner and the Baby Ruth packing crates it tossed with abandon.

PROJECT 12

Operating Cattle Car No. 3656

I f you had to choose one word to describe the world of postwar Lionel trains, it might be "action." The creative designers at Lionel made a series of cars and accessories that went a step beyond simply running a train in a circle. You could load or unload freight, launch a rocket to the moon, or transport cattle to the packing plant. One such car is the no. 3656 operating cattle car.

Introduced in 1949 as a follow-up to the milk car, the no. 3656 created a diversion along the main line. As with the milk car, the action took place on an elevated trackside platform. Nine little black cows could be made to "walk" in and out of the two overhead doors near the ends of the car. The trackside action was fascinating.

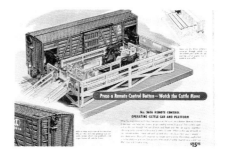

If kids love milk cans being thrown from reefers, they'd really love cows moving in and out of a stockcar—at least that was Lionel's thinking in 1949. And in fact, though it's not nearly as reliable as the milk car, the cattle car is fun to watch.

The no. 3656 was never as popular as the milk car, however, probably because it didn't function as reliably. The operating mechanism was more complicated and tended to go out of adjustment easily, causing bovine blockades at the doorway. Considering their final destination, I suppose they were naturally reluctant to enter the car.

How It Works

The cows usually managed to leave the car without difficulty. The bridge was slightly tilted, so the cows had gravity on their side. Cows entering the car, though, had a hill to climb. The design probably didn't start out that way, but it is a long way from the drafting table to the layout.

Vibration of the floating floor of the platform and runway in the car produced the motion of the cows in the car and corral. This shaking was made by solenoids: one mounted in the car floor and

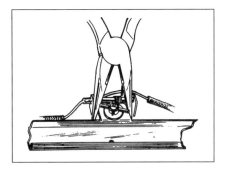

Fig. 1. Adjusting the plunger will ensure maximum vibration of the mechanism.

another beneath the platform. For best results, the unit should be connected to a source of variable voltage, such as the track, set between 12 and 15 volts of power. Because of the circuit design, it is important that the control switch be inserted on the "hot" or third-rail side and connected to the insulated terminal stud on the platform.

You can use either O or O-27 track with this accessory. Power blades of two different sizes and a special grounding clip for O gauge came with it. Four tabs on the sub-base and eight slots in the platform base provide vertical adjustments to compensate for the differences in rail height. A thumb nut at the rear holds the two bases together. The rails must seat firmly into one of two sets of notches in the sub-base. The lower set is for O-27, the upper set for O gauge. You will need older O-27 track sections for this to work right, as the tie flanges on newer track get in the way.

There are two versions of the no. 3656. The 1949 version had a slightly different platform, which was suspended by four grommeted tips resting on the fence, rather than on three pads. Instead of having a simple screw-type vibration adjustment, the 1949 model had an adjustment nut underneath, which necessitated resting the platform on blocks and turning it with a socket wrench. While the basic theories apply to both, the

later model is easier to work on and the more common, so this is what I'll use as my example.

The most likely source of operating trouble is the little sponge pads in the car and under the loading platform. They deteriorate, some hardening and others crumbling to dust. They invariably need to be replaced. Although Lionel apparently used the same pads for both car and platform, many parts dealers are providing two different types. The replacement pads for the car are softer than those for the platform, and it works better this way.

Pad replacement usually means adjustment of the bridge alignment and platform vibration. You may also need to make adjustments within the car. Let's take the procedure one step at a time.

Examining the Car

The carbody is held in place by one screw on each end. Remove the body from the frame and then check the door pivots. They need to be loose, so make sure the door assembly still pivots freely on the groove pins in the ends of the car. Warpage will sometimes cause it to scrape or bind, so use a file or sandpaper to ease the trouble spots.

Check the sliding door and cattle keeper arm assembly on the other side. It should be tight; otherwise it might be pushed open by the motion of the cattle, making it impossible to load the car.

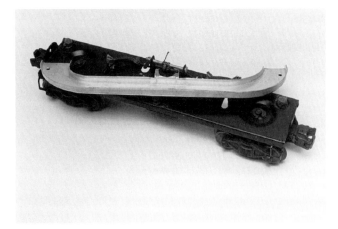

Fig. 2. Move the cattle runway to reach the car's sponge rubber pads.

Fig. 3. Pry off the pads and be sure all residue is removed.

Fig. 4. Place the new sponge in the same place as the old one.

Fig. 5. A little adhesive will ensure that the new pads remain in place.

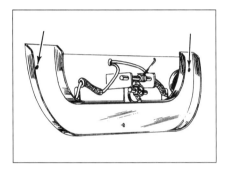

Fig. 6. Use the cattle runway's sighting holes to align the deck correctly.

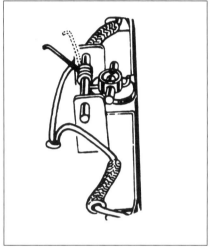

Fig. 7. Bend the spring upward to adjust the door lever.

Test the solenoid by applying 12 to 15 volts directly to the contact shoes on the trucks. It should buzz loudly at that voltage, which is considered optimum. If it does not buzz, check for broken, bare, or otherwise shorted wires between the trucks and the solenoid. If the insulation has deteriorated or hardened, replace with supple stranded wire. These solenoids rarely burn out, but if that should happen, you'll have to replace it with one that works from a junk car.

Occasionally, a tight solenoid plunger may result in poor vibration and sluggish door operation. This can usually be corrected by realigning the plunger within its supporting tube. As in fig. 1, carefully twist the plunger with pliers until maximum vibration is achieved.

Replace the old rubber pads. As shown in fig. 2, this can normally be done without removing the runway—just push it aside.

Then, as in fig. 3, clean off the pads and all their residue from the three indentations in the car floor.

Install the replacement pads, as seen in fig. 4, within their indented floor seats. These pads are supposed to be self-adhesive, but I like to use a little Walthers Goo under them, just the same (fig. 5). Goo is a type of contact cement that is safe for rubber and plastic.

Once you've cemented the pads in place and given them an hour or so to dry, the runway can be realigned. Original pads had holes in them, which could be matched up with the three holes in the runway for easy alignment. Replacement pads don't, so this becomes a bit tricky.

The ends of the runway should protrude an equal distance over the edge of the car floor. Figure 6 shows the correct alignment of the ramp. Center the runway carefully so that it won't interfere with plunger movement. When you have the runway lined up, put a dot of Goo on the top of each pad to fix it in place. When dry, carefully clean the runway with a cotton swab dipped in mineral spirits. This will remove the Goo that seeped up through the holes and any other dirt that might be on it.

Reassemble the Car

Make sure that the overhead doors still function satisfactorily. They should rise just enough to clear the cattle, yet still completely close. Their movement is controlled by a spring lever attached to the plunger. After pad replacement, the spring lever may need adjustment. As fig. 7 shows, try bending it up first. It may take a few tries to get it perfect. If the coil lead wires get in the way of the spring lever, tape them to the floor.

Platform Maintenance

Lift the platform from the base. The platform was originally plated for smoothness, so the surface should again be made as smooth and free of dirt and oxidation as possible. I usually use automotive chrome polish for this. Sometimes, bad areas also need a few passes with a Scotch-Brite pad. Follow that up with WD-40 and wipe the area dry in order to stop any rust.

Name and Number: Operating cattle car no. 3656 and platform.

General maintenance: Solenoids and the bridges between car and corral need occasional adjustment. Keep power pickup shoes clean, and the car and platform free of oil, dust, and dirt. The runway inside the car and the corral platform needs to be smooth. Shine with Scotch-Brite pad if necessary.

Maintenance schedule: As needed.

Troubleshooting:

1. Car solenoid doesn't work—Check wires for damage or bad insulation.

2. Platform solenoid doesn't work—Check internal wiring and contacts.

3. Platform and/or car vibration insufficient to move cattle—Replace the six sponge rubber pads (three in car, three under platform). Readjust the vibration solenoids and spring lever with new pads in place until car and corral vibrations match.

4. Entry and exit doors won't open—Check end pivots. If doors are warped, sand or file lightly until they pivot freely.

5. Cattle won't stay in car—Tighten keeper arm on sliding door.

6. Cattle refuse to enter (or exit) car correctly—Adjust bridge tabs by bending them slightly until the action is satisfactory and cattle move smoothly.

Adjust the hinges on the four plastic gates, if needed. They should seat firmly in both the open and closed position.

Note the position of the three rubber pads as seen in fig. 8. Scrape off all residue before you install the new ones. As with the car pads, cement them in place with Goo, but only on the bottom. The platform must remain removable.

After you've replaced the pads, the platform bridge will need readjustment. This is best done with the platform and front fence section removed. The car should be in

Fig. 8. (Top) As with pads on the car, be sure to place corral pads in the exact position shown.

Fig. 9. (Above) Adjust the screw downward for good platform vibration.

Fig. 10. (Above right) If all else fails, resort to the manual pinkie poke method of loading the car.

place on the track. When lowered, the ramps must line up with the level of the cattle runway in the car for smooth loading or unloading.

Holding the bridge connecting bar with pliers, adjust the cattle entrance ramp (right side, facing the car) to the precise height of the runway. Then bend the finger at the back of the ramp so that it just touches the floor of the platform when the bridge is lowered.

Adjust the exit ramp (left side, facing the car) in the same way. It is very important that at least one of the ramp fingers makes contact with the floor of the platform at all times. That is how the floor vibration is transmitted to the bridge. Since the ramp alignment is more

critical at the car entrance, many technicians rely on the exit ramp finger for this contact.

Excessive platform vibration can be reduced by turning the adjusting screw downward upon the coil armature beneath it (fig. 9). The idea is to get the platform and the car vibrating at about the same rate.

The 3656 cattle cars and platform corrals have been known to work well together when new or recently serviced or adjusted. Soon after, they begin to develop individual personality quirks that impede their smooth, tandem effort. Keeping them tweaked to perform in unison can eat many valuable maintenance hours.

So you can either take the time to ensure it works smoothly, or you can do what thousands of kids did back in the 1950s. When their heifers refused to board the portable cow palace, they gave the cantankerous critters encouragement. A quick pinkie poke in the rump roast usually did the trick to get them "moooving."

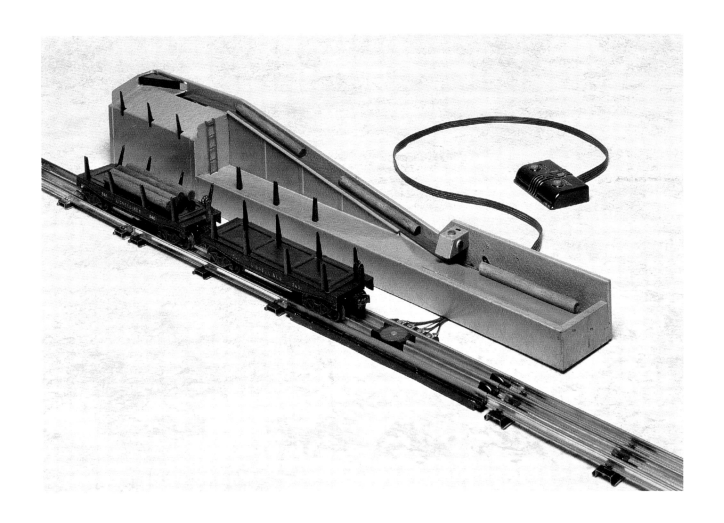

PROJECT 13

Lumber Loader No. 364

The no. 364 conveyor belt lumber loader was a highly popular trackside accessory that was in production for 10 years, from 1948 to 1957. Designed for use with the nos. 3451 and 3461 operating lumber cars, it could be made to work with later cars as well. Because it depended on only one heavy-duty motor and the law of gravity for successful operation, no. 364 turned out to be one of Lionel's most reliable performers.

The no. 364 conveyor lumber loader was a favorite of many postwar youngsters. Cataloged from 1948 to 1957, the device made lots of noise, had a light on it, and created motion—Lionel's tried and true formula for accessory success.

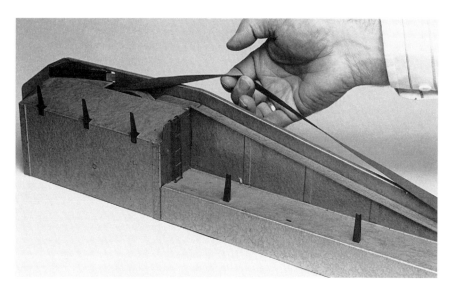

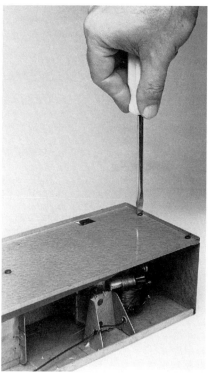

Fig. 1. After being stored for years in a position that stretches it, the belt is of no use to anyone and will need to be replaced before the accessory will operate as it should.

Fig. 2. Disassembly is simple, requiring only a screwdriver to remove the sheet-metal back of the accessory. With the back removed, the loader's inner workings are readily accessible for maintenance.

How It Works

The lower end of the lumber loader must be positioned next to a remote-control track section so the logs can be dumped into it automatically. When the motor is started, the logs are moved by the conveyor belt to the high end, where they roll one by one onto an empty car waiting on the same track. Kids who had only one car moved it a few inches down the track to the other end of the accessory before they started the motor. The action was pointless, but fun to watch—for a while.

A low-hooded floodlight, which burns continuously, illuminates the receiving area so the loader can be used at night. Green lenses on both sides of the hood are apparently there to help the engineer spot his car from either direction. The purpose of the red lens on the top eludes me. The thing isn't high enough to pose a hazard to navigation, so it can't be of much concern to aircraft in the area.

The mechanism is simple. The motor, coupled to a reduction gearbox, slowly turns the large pulley that drives the belt. This motor/gearbox/pulley assembly is pivoted and spring-loaded to maintain the proper tension on the belt. A belt-operated cam at the lower end jostles the floor to keep the logs moving onto the belt.

When the logs reach the high end of the loader, gravity takes over. They slide off the belt, roll rapidly down an inclined plane, and land on top of the car or whatever else may be on the track at that moment. The three stakes on the high end aren't intended to hold the logs in place. Their only purpose is to extend the path of the rolling logs far enough so they're deposited on, not next to, the waiting flatcar.

Service

The motor needs frequent maintenance. Because the motor is suspended upside down, liquefied gearbox lubricant tends to run into it during extended operation, fouling both the brushes and commutator. For that reason, I don't recommend relubricating the gearbox unless it sounds labored and noisy. And then do it sparingly. I don't know what Lionel put in there 40 years ago, but the stuff just keeps on working.

In repairing one of these accessories, I usually find the conveyor belt needs to be replaced. A combination of hard use and improper storage can cause the belt to stretch beyond its useful limits (fig. 1). Check it by running the accessory. The belt should ride flat, without wandering from side to side or slipping. Little ripples on the edges are sure signs of stretching. Good-quality replacements are available.

To replace the belt, remove the sheet-metal screws that hold the backplates in place (fig. 2). Starting at the low end, follow the path of the old belt as you install the new one. The three belt rollers and cam are held in place by pins that can be pulled out when the backplates are removed. Take these out one at a time as you thread the new belt through its course. Put one small drop of oil on each pin before you reinsert it. One drop is helpful; more is way too much.

To improve the belt's traction, Lionel wrapped a length of cloth tape around the drive pulley. After long use, the tape becomes smooth, thereby losing some of its

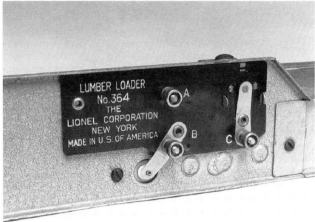

Fig. 3. **(Above and above right)** To improve belt traction, lightly roughen the factory-applied cloth tape with fine sandpaper. Don't overdo it; just scratch it enough to give the belt a little tooth.

Name and Number: Lumber loader no. 364

General maintenance: Motor needs frequent cleaning because gearbox lubricant drips into it. Keep belt and upper surfaces free from oil, dust, and dirt. Don't oil gearbox unless motor sounds labored; don't oil belt rollers unless they squeak.

Maintenance schedule: As needed.

Troubleshooting:

1. Motor doesn't run—Check for broken wires, sticking brushes, or dirty commutator.

2. Motor runs slowly—Needs cleaning.

3. Belt slips—Bend motor pivot spring to increase tension. Roughen surface of main pulley with fine sandpaper. Replace belt if it's stretched.

4. Stakes at high end stick—Check for bent stake shaft. Too much play in pivot, causing motor to press against stake shaft; insert thrust washer.

5. Logs fall off too quickly—Shim front of ramp so logs remain against back of ramp until they reach the triangular stop.

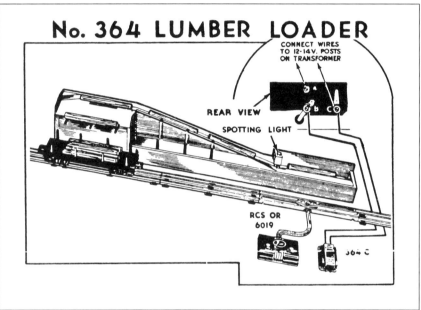

Fig. 4. Hookup is simple, as the instruction sheet illustrates it. Transformer leads from any two 12- to 14-volt posts go to A and C on the back of the accessory. The accessory also requires a no. 364C controller to turn it on and off. Wires from posts B and C go to A and B on the underside of the 364C controller. A UCS track is required for dumping the logs from an operating flatcar to the lower bin of the accessory.

effectiveness. Roughen it slightly with medium-grit sandpaper before installing the new belt. See fig. 3. If the belt still slips, roughen it some more. (It's normal for the new belt to slip a little when the splice runs under the cam roller. This condition will go away as the belt wears in.)

I don't recommend trying to replace the pulley tape because the old stuff doesn't come off easily, and I have no idea what on today's market is equal to the task. Like the gearbox lubricant, Lionel's tape was intended to last forever.

Another common cause of belt slippage can be traced to the spring that's wound around the motor/gearbox/pulley assembly pivot. It can lose some of its tension over time. Bend the ends of this spring so that it exerts maximum pressure on the belt when the accessory is in the normal operating position.

Operation/Collectibility

For best results, the loader should always rest on a level surface. It's intended to operate at between 12 and 14 volts and should be hooked up to an appropriate fixed-voltage circuit on your transformer. The transformer

This accessory has never made a lot of sense in terms of operation. If you'd like to add a little bit of reason, however, consider using it as an "intermodal" accessory—from rail to truck.

leads are connected to binding posts A and C, as shown in fig. 4. The 364C controller (or any other on/off switch) is connected between binding posts B and C. This way, the light will burn continu- ously, and the motor will be con- trolled by the switch.

Variations are few. The motors on the earlier models had the old tube-type brushplates. Later versions are usually found with the redesigned "tubeless" ones. The changeover probably took place at the turn of the 1950s. The 364 is known to have been produced only in gray, with either a crackle or hammertone finish. One source also reports a shiny finish. This may or may not repre- sent a third variation. More likely it's a semantic distinction, describ- ing the hammertone finish in con- trast to the crackle.

This accessory is almost cer- tainly more fun to operate than to collect, even though the logs go nowhere fast.

Bascule Bridge No. 313

Lionel's no. 313 bascule bridge was the masterpiece of a production period celebrated for automated marvels and advancements in toy train engineering. Unlike most of the other accessories produced in the late prewar era, this O gauge bridge has a realistic appearance and operation like that of counterbalanced drawbridges, which raise on one end when the other is lowered.

The bascule bridge was introduced in 1940 and, except for the war years, remained cataloged through 1949. Because the length of its Bakelite span is equivalent to two sections of Lionel OS straight track, no. 313 fits into almost any O gauge layout. It works for O-27 too, though at least one straight section must be cut to fit.

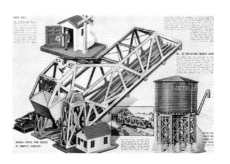

Lionel's no. 313 bascule bridge has been bringing excitement and fun to O gauge layouts for more than half a century since being introduced in the 1940 catalog.

Up and Down, Stop and Start

How does the bascule bridge operate and where can problems set in? Press the controller button, and the span slowly rises to its zenith (16″ above track level), then returns to the lowered position in an uninterrupted cycle. While the span is up, track power is shut off to prevent trains from running toward an open bridge.

To automatically stop trains approaching an open bridge, runs of at least four track sections should extend from both sides of the bridge. These sections must be insulated from the rest of the layout by inserting fiber pins into the center rails.

In addition, locomotives with traditional E-units must be locked into the "forward only" position to function with the automatic stop/start feature.

The fixed-voltage circuit that powers the bridge must be completely independent of the track circuit. The bridge mechanism is designed to operate on about 14 volts; some require slightly less.

Motor and Gearbox

The noise produced by an operating bridge is more than just esthetic. The small motor works very hard, particularly if the counterbalance spring isn't properly adjusted. This motor is undersized for the job, so it needs

Fig. 1. The undersized motor installed on the bascule bridge must do some real "power lifting" to raise the span.

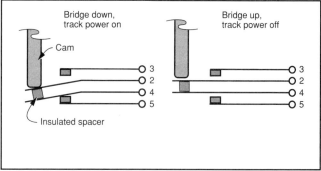

Fig. 2. By interrupting power to the track, the four-layer wafer-switch prevents trains from running off an open bridge.

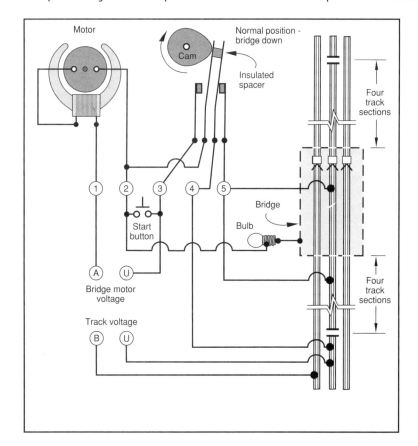

Fig. 3. This expanded wiring diagram illustrates motor and warning light connections missing from the original instruction sheet schematic of the no. 313 bascule bridge.

Fig. 4. The bridge's counterbalance spring is the key to smooth and efficient operation. The adjustment screw is located under the structure, so it's best to make adjustments before installing the bridge.

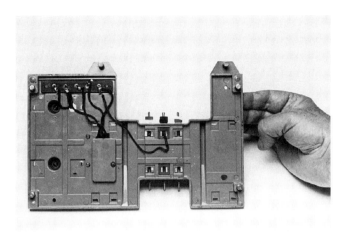

Fig. 5. The view from beneath the bridge base reveals the hole for the spring adjustment screw. Note the wiring from the binding posts to the motor and track.

Fig. 6. A "flood damaged" bridge. The base of this Lionel bascule bridge has warped; filing and/or shimming the base may correct this problem.

regular maintenance to prevent it from burning out. Keeping the armature shaft lubricated on both ends, the commutator face shiny, and the slots cleaned helps the motor operate efficiently (fig. 1).

The reduction gear train, located between the house and superstructure, is installed in a die-cast enclosure that's difficult to reach. Fortunately, it was packed with grease at the Lionel factory and usually isn't a problem. An occasional drop of oil on the ends of the protruding shafts is all that's required.

If you have to disassemble the mechanism, it wouldn't hurt to grease the gears. Remove the three screws at the top, and the box comes apart.

Electrical Circuitry

Two electrical circuits are associated with the bridge's operation. Both of them pass through a four-layer wafer-switch attached to the bottom of the gear shafts. This switch allows the bridge to run through its operational cycle while trains wait for it to conclude. Using a clever yet simple mechanism, the switch is activated by a rotating cam fixed on the end of a gear shaft.

As fig. 2 shows, when the bridge is down, the cam exerts pressure on the switch and closes the circuit between the bottom two layers. These layers are connected to binding posts 4 and 5, which control power to the insulated track blocks on both sides of

the bridge. In this position, the track power is on, allowing trains to pass through.

Because the cam is fixed to the end of a gear shaft, it rotates while the bridge is in motion and relinquishes the pressure exerted on the switch. Accordingly, the switch springs back into its normal position (fig. 2), which shuts off the track power and closes the contacts between the upper two layers. These layers are connected to binding posts 2 and 3 and control the power to the bridge motor.

When the cycle ends, the cam exerts pressure on the switch again. The accessory motor then stops, and trains move across the bridge span.

To begin the cycle, it's necessary to start the motor while the cam still rests on the switch. For that purpose, a push button provides a temporary shunt or current bridge between binding posts 2 and 3. This lets the motor run long enough for the cam to move off the switch.

The switch can be reached by removing the three screws that hold the gear housing in place. Removing them from the bottom of the base lets you move the housing just enough to reach the switch. Be careful not to break off the wires.

Because the switch contacts are exposed, they collect dirt and require occasional cleaning. I recommend squirting a little TV tuner cleaner on them or swabbing a

pipe cleaner dipped in mineral spirits between contact points.

You can check the condition of the switch contacts by performing three continuity tests using a volt-ohm-milliammeter or a similar instrument. (You can also use two wires from a transformer.) If you get a spark when you touch the binding posts in question, there's continuity.

First, when the bridge is down, there should be continuity between binding posts 4 and 5. (These are connected to the lower pair of contacts, which should be closed while the cam is resting on the switch.) There should not be continuity between binding posts 2 and 3.

Second, when the bridge is up, there should be continuity between binding posts 2 and 3. (These are connected to the upper pair of contacts, which should be closed while the cam isn't resting on the switch.) There should not be continuity between binding posts 4 and 5.

Third, when the bridge is in either position, there shouldn't be continuity between binding posts 2 and 4. If there is, the insulating spacer is missing. Replace it with the spacer from any RCS or UCS track controller (part no. RCS-27).

If the switch passes all three tests, it's functioning properly. If not, you have to flex and bend the layers until it does.

Wiring Diagram

Lionel wired the red light on top of the bridge directly to the

Name and Number: Bascule bridge no. 313

General maintenance: Small motor requires frequent tune-ups. Lubricate exposed motor and gearbox shafts with one drop of oil. Clean switch contacts with a little TV tuner cleaner. Wipe dust, dirt, and excess oil from all exposed surfaces.

Maintenance schedule: At least once a year; more if bridge is used extensively.

Troubleshooting:

1. Motor doesn't run—Check wiring diagram for proper hookup. Check wiring from binding posts to motor and layer switch.

2. Motor runs too slowly—Needs tune-up

3. Motor runs unevenly, slower on upward cycle than downward—Adjust counterbalance spring.

4. Motor doesn't shut off at the end of cycle—Look for loose cam or faulty switch contacts.

5. Track power doesn't shut off when the span is raised or return when it's lowered—Look for loose cam or faulty switch contacts.

6. Span is canted in the lowered position—Adjust the uprights and/or shim the base to compensate for warpage.

7. Lamp replacement—Bulb no. 1456, 18-volt clear bayonet base.

track voltage, so it burns continuously while a train runs. I prefer to use mine as a warning device, with the light switching on as the bridge goes up and remaining on until it lowers. To accomplish this neat effect, I moved the lamp lead wire to the solder terminal under binding post 2. I added this modification to the wiring diagram (fig. 3).

The diagram is based on one drawn for no. 313's instruction sheet. I've expanded the original diagram by illustrating the wiring beyond the connection to the five binding posts on the terminal strip. This information comes in handy when you're servicing a bascule bridge.

Note that Lionel's diagram shows the track voltage wires reversed from their normal positions (the "ground" is on the third rail, and the "hot" side is on the running rails). This shouldn't cause any problems unless you have a large layout with a common ground and complex circuitry. If you do, experiment by switching wires until you find the right combination.

Counterbalance Spring

A properly adjusted spring contributes to the efficient operation of Lionel's bascule bridge. These springs tend to lose some resilience over time, particularly if the bridge happened to be stored with its spring extended. Be sure to make any initial adjustments before placing the bridge into service (fig. 4).

Though necessary, adjusting the counterbalance spring in the course of normal operation is difficult, especially if the bridge is installed on a permanent layout. Unfortunately, the long screw used to adjust the counterbalance is accessible only from the bottom of the base. I recommend drilling a hole in the benchwork under the adjusting screw so you can reach it from below (fig. 5).

The *Lionel Service Manual* does not indicate how to measure the spring tension. However, common sense dictates that proper adjustment comes at the point where the upward and downward motions are equally fluid.

The spring should extend far enough to minimize the strain on the motor while the bridge rises, but not so far that it prevents the bridge from resting firmly in the lowered position. Inertia and gravity notwithstanding, the speed of the upward and downward cycles should appear to be the same. The sound of the motor also indicates how well a bridge is balanced. It shouldn't sound much more labored on the upward cycle than on the down.

Bridge over Troubled Water

The bascule bridge was designed for use with O or O-27 track. To compensate for the higher O gauge track profile, four hexagonal screws must be inserted into the corners of the base. Unfortunately, if these screws are left in place when the unit is stored, the weight of the bridge eventually causes the base to warp. This condition is compounded if the counterbalance spring is also extended.

As a result, it's difficult to find a 313 that isn't somewhat worse for wear or storage (fig. 6). Almost all bases show some signs of warpage. If, however, the warpage isn't severe, it can be compensated by filing and/or shimming the base during installation. In an extreme case, the base may need to be drilled and screwed to the benchwork. The screw holes should be located in positions where the base is "high." Once inserted, the screws exert pressure that bends the base to compensate for some of the warpage. Do this judiciously—the die-cast bases are thin and can break.

The goal is to make the base as level and the uprights as vertical as possible. If they're crooked, the bridge lowers at an angle. Sight along the rails and adjust the base until the bridge rails are aligned with the approach track. Your patience will be rewarded many times over in smooth and reliable operation of your bascule bridge. If, however, the base can't be satisfactorily corrected, install beveled wood block "guides" next to the approach track to align the span as it lowers.

Like real bridges, Lionel's bascule bridge is subject to stresses and mechanical difficulties. To minimize the effect of most stresses, it's probably best to permanently install the bridge on your layout. Maintenance won't be much more difficult; better still, the realistic sights and sounds of an operating bascule bridge will delight your visitors!

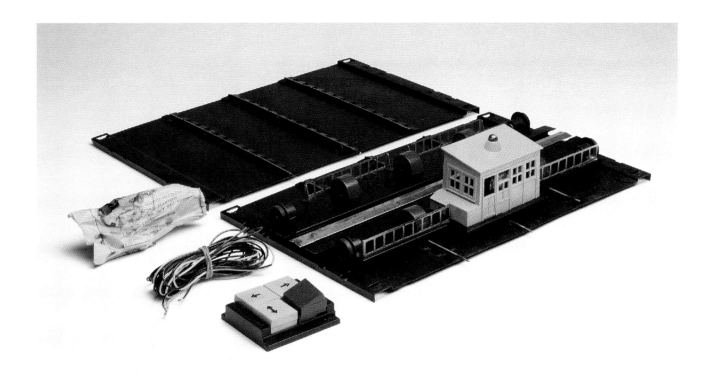

PROJECT 15

Transfer Table No. 350

Lionel's transfer table was introduced in 1957, at a time when many prototype railroads were replacing their aging turntables. Transfer tables were more efficient with space, easier to maintain, and, with the advent of dieselization, it was no longer necessary to turn locomotives at the end of each trip.

Like most Lionel accessories, the transfer table can be great fun to operate. The motor roars and grinds authoritatively and the ready light blinks on and off. Although the table moves at an appropriately slow speed, there are no built-in stops, so a certain level of acquired operator skill is needed to get the rails to line up correctly. Often the control has to be rocked back and forth several times. Theoretically, the locomotive can't draw power to run unless the table and the approach track are perfectly aligned. However, it is possible to run your diesel engine into the pit in spite of this failsafe system. (See, I told you this accessory could be fun!)

This interesting accessory from 1957, the no. 350 transfer table, is hard to find, but it's easy to operate and delightful to watch.

At approximately 70 scale feet in length, the Lionel transfer table was designed to accommodate the largest single unit diesel locomotive then available (or a very short steamer). Double unit diesels had to be moved one at a time unless two tables were connected end-to-end. This was possible, but didn't work so very well because it was hard to get the two drive motors synchronized well enough to function reliably in tandem.

A total of four approach tracks, two on each end, could be attached to the rail-bed base of the accessory. Brackets and adapters were provided to accommodate O, Super-O, and O-27 track. Additional bases, each with the potential for adding four more tracks to extend the table's run, were available separately.

Although cataloged from 1957 to 1960, the transfer table apparently wasn't a big seller. Sales figures are not available, but I don't see many on the used train market today. I suppose that's because of the amount of layout space it required for the table itself and tracks on which to park the engines. This discouraged many table top operators from buying it. Since no major variations have been noted, this also suggests there may have been only one production run.

How It Works

The locomotive may board the transfer table from any of the four attached tracks and exit on any of the other three. The tracks are aligned so that it is possible to run the engine straight across the accessory to the opposite side without moving the table.

As the locomotive rolls onto the table, its motor becomes a low resistance in parallel with the shack's lamp, and the roof light dims or goes out. The controller light remains on, but the locomotive can't draw enough current to run. Pressing the power button shorts the lamp and sends full voltage to the locomotive.

A two-button rocker switch controls the direction of travel. This switch is designed and pivoted in such a way that both forward and reverse circuits can't be energized at the same time.

Electrical Connections

The "hot" (third-rail) power lead is connected to terminal D on the controller. All circuits are grounded through the base of the accessory and the track is attached to it.

The black lead is connected to the left-hand rail on the accessory base and terminal A on the controller. This supplies the power to move the table forward. The yellow lead goes to the right-hand rail and terminal C on the controller. This connection enables the table to move backward. The red lead is connected to the center rail and terminal B. It provides power to the center rail on the table itself, which in turn feeds power to the waiting locomotive.

The center rail on the accessory base is positioned within an insulating strip, with a flange extending above it. The contact shoe under the transfer table can touch this rail only at the two places where there are notches in the flange. These notches correspond with the positions of the approach tracks.

Connections to the accessory base are made with small plugs (the size of an O-27 track pin) inserted into the ends of the tubular rails. Push these plugs all the way in or the transfer table will hit them and short out.

Powering the Accessory

You can power the accessory by using the track voltage. Connect terminal D on the controller to the center rail terminal clip on the track lockon or to the transformer binding post feeding that terminal.

You may also use separate variable voltage sources for the transfer table and the main line. This enables the accessory to be controlled independently from the rest of the layout. It requires a Lionel KW, ZW, or separate trans-

Most transfer table motors are low mileage and should perform well with an occasional clean-up/tune-up and minimal maintenance.

former (fixed-voltage hookups don't work well with transfer tables, for obvious reasons.)

Routine Maintenance

The transfer table is quite sturdy and relatively trouble-free. With heavy sheet-metal construction throughout and a large motor and gearbox, it was built to last. Ours survived at least one flood at Madison Hardware and kept right on ticking. This is a case where Lionel's engineers overdesigned this one!

The gearboxes were lubed at the factory and may still be OK. Lionel used some good lubricants in the 1950s. Check out yours. A few drops of oil through the hole on top was all ours needed to smooth itself out.

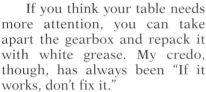

Minor corrosion damage can be repaired with plastic steel epoxy in three easy steps. Clean it, apply epoxy, and sand it.

First apply the epoxy with a stick. Remove excess epoxy with a putty knife so the surface you're repairing is smooth before it dries.

Let the epoxy dry for two days. Gently sand with both medium- and fine-grit sandpaper. Use gun blue to tint the bare metal.

If you think your table needs more attention, you can take apart the gearbox and repack it with white grease. My credo, though, has always been "If it works, don't fix it."

Transfer tables usually fall into the low-mileage category. Chances are the motors on most transfer tables have not be subjected to hard, extended operation that causes commutator faces to foul and brushes to stick. However, if this happens, the motor may be cleaned in the usual way.

The table's four wheel bearings should be oiled occasionally, with one or two drops on each.

It is important to keep the three sprung contact shoes on the underside of the table and rails upon which they ride free of dirt, oxidation, and corrosion.

Plastic Steel Epoxy Saves the Day

The base of my transfer table had some corrosion damage that I decided to repair myself using plastic steel epoxy.

There are dozens of applications around the train room for this handy product, a compound that contains powdered metal. You will find it's easy to use, dries hard within 24 hours, and may be shaped into almost any configuration with a file or sandpaper. The metal in the compound makes repairs strong and durable. I've used it often to rebuild chipped or broken driver flanges. Once it bonds, it stays put and wears well. Unfortunately, it does not conduct electricity.

Several brands of plastic steel epoxy are on the market, and while they are all quite similar, it is still advisable to carefully follow the directions on the individual package. With the dual-syringe dispenser, only the amount required to do a particular job need be mixed. The rest can be capped and stored for future use.

I chose this particular product brand to fill in the pitted spots on the transfer table base because of its color match. Almost any other epoxy compound could have been used, but it would have to be painted to blend with the chemically blackened areas around it.

First, I filed and sanded the rusty and pitted areas, making sure that the unaffected metal around the pits was as smooth and level as possible.

I then washed the area to be treated with a detergent solution and rinsed it thoroughly under running water to remove all the sanding debris and any oily residue. A clean and dry metal base is essential for a good bond.

After mixing an appropriate amount of plastic steel epoxy, I applied it liberally over the entire area, with a disposable stick. I removed the excess epoxy with a putty knife and generally smoothed over the repair. I made sure that a thin layer of the epoxy covered the entire treated area, not just the pitted areas.

I gave the epoxy two days to completely dry. I sanded the repaired area, using medium-grit emery paper followed by fine-grit paper until I was down to bare metal all around the epoxy fills. When the affected area was as smooth as it could be, I reblackened the bare metal with two applications of liquid gun blue.

As a finishing touch, I rubbed the entire base with a cloth dipped in WD-40. This blended in the repaired areas. The result was certainly quite satisfactory and a lot better than trying to live with damage that can be so easily repaired.

Lionel created a dandy accessory when it made the no. 350. It was not only well built, but it was as modern as the diesel locomotives it carried. It also generated light, noise, and movement! What more could a kid have asked for? If you are lucky enough to own one, and you follow these simple maintenance steps, you can expect your transfer table to work reliably for a long time.

Magnet Cranes Nos. 165 and 182

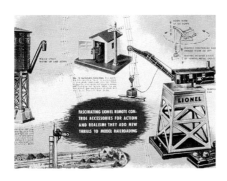

Lionel's magnet cranes nos. 165 and 182 are ingenious devices that are as easy to fix as they are fun to operate.

The Lionel Corp.'s magnet crane was the most fascinating train-related toy of its day. Unlike so many other accessories that had only two modes (on and off), the nos. 165 and later 182 cranes were operator dependent and required the development of hand-eye coordination to run them well. Magnet cranes were designed to handle miniature scrap iron pieces. This gave them an almost infinite variety of moves when loading and unloading freight cars.

Fig. 1. The power behind (or rather, underneath) the magnet crane. Preventive maintenance is your crane's key to happiness.

Fig. 2. Follow this highlighted path when you restring the boom and magnet assembly. Leave enough string on the spool to allow the magnet a ground-level reach.

Control and Function

Four buttons and a rotary switch provide remote control for all the crane's functions. The cab and boom can be rotated 360 degrees, and the block and tackle can move up or down, all by pressing the appropriate buttons. The rotary switch energizes the magnet and powers a red light in the cab simultaneously. The boom is raised or lowered manually by turning a wheel on the back of the cab.

Lionel recommended an operating voltage for the crane that ranged between 10 and 16 volts.

Service and Repair

The small motor requires frequent service. The commutator face and slots, as well as the brushes and brush holders, should be cleaned periodically. Unless these parts are damaged beyond repair, they'll be cleaned adequately by a few squirts of TV tuner cleaner from Radio Shack. Don't forget to oil the armature shaft.

Since the crane's gears and clutches are well made, they rarely require anything more than basic lubrication. Grease them and any other moving parts whenever you clean the motor.

The clutch solenoids are another matter. They're prone to the troubles most often associated with such devices—sticky plungers and broken wires. If your crane's plunger is sticking, spritz some TV tuner cleaner directly into the hole and work it back and forth until it's free. *Never* lubricate solenoid plungers. Lubricants attract dirt, and dirt makes plungers stick.

If the solenoids on your crane refuse to operate, check the wires. Are they still attached at both ends? Because they're protected, they rarely break off from their terminals. If yours have broken free, solder them back into place. Burned-out solenoids must be rewound or replaced with parts from a swap meet "junker."

Because of operator abuse, it's common to encounter solenoid and motor burnout in Lionel magnet cranes. The controller buttons are designed to be pressed individually, but it's possible to combine functions by pushing two buttons simultaneously. For example, you can press *left* or *right* and *down* together, but any other combination will cause trouble. Young operators quickly discovered this shorthand method, but such discoveries came with the price of wrong button-pushing. Incorrect combinations of buttons stall the motor and send the solenoids into heated spasms.

The magnet crane's cab can make any number of complete circular revolutions in either direction. To accomplish this feat, Lionel designed an ingenious system to transmit power from the fixed base to the electromagnet and the cab light using two shafts.

One shaft is attached to the block and tackle take-up spool within the cab. It's hollow and *very* fragile. Another shaft is mounted coaxially and is insulated from the first shaft. Brass finger contacts on both the moving cab and fixed base assembly provide continuous electrical contact regardless of the crane's position or movement. These contacts must be kept clean and adjusted occasionally to maintain adequate pressure against the ends of the shaft.

If the red light inside the cab has burned out, replace it with an 18-volt, bayonet-base bulb (Lionel's original part was no. 165-53). To install a bulb in a no. 165 crane, gently squeeze the sides of the cab until the roof pops off. The cab on a no. 182 is held in place by two screws at the rear of the housing. Remove them, unscrew the boom height-control wheel, and lift away the housing.

The Magnet and the String

Take a good look at the magnet and its wiring. When you turn the rotary switch on the controller, an electrical charge is sent through the cable, energizing the electromagnet. In spite of its apparent fragility, this assembly is rarely found in bad condition. If

Name and Number: Magnet cranes nos. 165 and 182

General maintenance: Keep accessory clean. Motor requires frequent service, using the tune-up hints from Chapter 1. Grease all moving parts—gears, bearings, and clutches—whenever motor is serviced.

Maintenance schedule: As required. Fairly often.

Troubleshooting: The most common cause of trouble is the six-conductor control cable hardwired between the control box and the accessory. The rubber insulation tends to harden with age and break away, causing short circuits that can result in all manner of malfunctions and erratic operation. *Always check the cable first.* Don't neglect that which is hidden from view inside the controller and under the metal hold-down bracket on the accessory base.

1. Motor doesn't work—Check for broken wires, burned-out or very dirty motor.

2. Cab doesn't rotate in both directions—Check clutch solenoids for broken wires, burned-out coils, and/or sticky plungers. Repair, replace, or unstick as needed.

3. Cable doesn't move up and down—Check the contacts on both ends of the coaxial control shaft. Clean and adjust.

4. Cab light doesn't go on—Check bulb. Check the contacts on both ends of the coaxial control shaft. Clean and adjust.

5. Magnet doesn't work—The magnet cable is a fragile, supple length of stranded wire. Check to see if it is broken at the magnet itself or in the cab. Resolder or replace.

6. Control cable on the block and tackle frayed or broken—Replace with heavy woven fishline.

7. Bulb—Lionel used an 18-volt red no. 165-53.

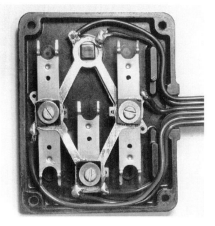

Fig. 3. Connect the wires between the controller (**above**) and the contact plate (**right**) on the underside of the crane's base. Use short wire leads and a minimum of solder during installation to avoid shorts. Make sure your six-conductor cable is flat.

the wires are broken from their connections, resolder them.

If the wiring is missing or can't be repaired, consult your Lionel parts dealer or Madison Hardware in Detroit. Or you can try using very supple, shielded phonograph pickup cable, available from some electronics stores.

The simulated cable (or "string," if you will) doesn't age well. In fact, if your crane still has its original string, it's probably quite fragile. I replace aging string with like-colored, supple-woven fishing line. As installed in Irvington, the string was knotted behind a hole in the spool. The spool was then tightly attached to the shaft.

This shaft is easily damaged, so don't remove the spool from it. Instead, glue about an inch of the fishing line around the spool with epoxy cement or a cyanoacrylate adhesive (CA). Run the line under the roller bar next to the spool, up the underside of the boom, over the top of the pulley at the end, through the hook assembly, and back through the little hole located about an inch from the end of the boom. Make sure there's enough line on the spool to lower the magnet to "ground level." Tie a double knot at the end of the fishing line. See fig. 2.

New Control Cable

The most common repair problem with a magnet crane involves the replacement of the six-conductor cable. The rubber Lionel used hardens, cracks, and rots away, leaving the wiring harness exposed and prone to short-ing. Fortunately, plastic replacement cable is available from Lionel parts dealers.

Replacing the cable isn't difficult, but you should work slowly and carefully. Label each wire's location at both ends of the harness before removing the old assembly. If the old wiring is missing, refer to fig. 3.

Remember, Lionel installed the original wiring harness so that it lay flat between the crane and controller. If yours is twisted, you've installed it incorrectly.

Use caution when you solder wires to the controller's wafer switch lugs. It's easy to accidentally create a bridge of wire or solder between the wafer layers. As a rule, keep the wire ends stripped short and use a minimum of solder.

Because these cranes are complex mechanisms, remember to pause and test each phase of your repair. Don't wait to test things until you've finished the entire job.

An Accessory Before Its Time

In the end you'll have a fully operational toy that was truly the Eighth Wonder of the World in the 1940s. The poor kids of today have no idea what fun they've been missing. Get your magnet crane into top shape and introduce them to this dynamite accessory.

PROJECT 17

Coal Elevator No. 97

Despite the furious activity it generates, Lionel's no. 97 coal elevator is a simple accessory. There are no complicated clutches or linkages, no imponderable wiring, and no critical adjustments. It only has one motor and two solenoids.

Switch it on and the motor lifts coal into the tower. Push a button and the coal dumps into a waiting gondola or hopper. Yes, that's all there is to it. (Controller missing? Build your own using the tips in Projects 6 and 7.)

Maintaining your no. 978 consists primarily of keeping it clean and lubricated. That makes it a great accessory for a "first" repair project. Even if you've never disassembled a Lionel train or accessory in your life, I encourage you to try your hand on old no. 97.

Transfer coal from one hopper to another hopper on the next track over with the no. 97 coal elevator. Why? C'mon, these are toy trains!

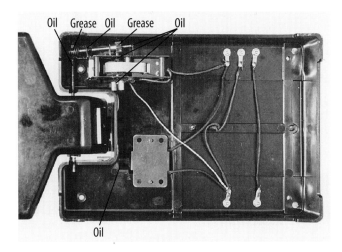

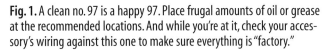

Fig. 1. A clean no. 97 is a happy 97. Place frugal amounts of oil or grease at the recommended locations. And while you're at it, check your accessory's wiring against this one to make sure everything is "factory."

Fig. 2. This screw is the key to smooth, bind-free operation. After loosening it, adjust the elevator structure until the chain mechanism flows freely.

Name and Number: Coal elevator no. 97
General maintenance: Keep accessory clean. Tune the motor, using the hints of motor tuning from Chapter 1.
Maintenance schedule: As needed. Motor will require frequent attention because the accessory is underpowered.
Troubleshooting:
1. Accessory dead—Check for broken wires, burned-out or very dirty motor.
2. Accessory jammed up—Look for stray lumps of "coal" that often get into the works.
3. Sluggish operation—Tune up motor. Lubricate all motor and gear shafts so that they turn freely. Sometimes, the motor bearing between the brushes gets very dry and "chatters" as it turns. Lubrication usually cures it.
4. Bin or chute solenoids inoperative—Check for broken wires, burned-out coils, and/or sticking plungers. Repair, replace, or unstick as required.
5. Bin solenoid binds—Loosen screw (shown in fig. 2) and move the elevator structure to the left or right until the bind is minimized or eliminated. Note: It is best not to lubricate the conveyor chain or chute gate. Artificial "coal" tends to stick to lubricants.

How It Works

Here's the deal: Start by placing no. 97 between parallel tracks 14¾" apart (measured between center rails). The "rear" track requires an uncoupling section (UCS or RCS) adjacent to the accessory. When you hit the UCS's "operate" button, a dump car unloads its shipment of coal into no. 97's scoop bin. Turn the elevator's motor on, the scoop bin lifts, and the chain-driven bucket mechanism carries coal to the tower. With a press of no. 97's unloading button, coal tumbles from the tower chute into an awaiting hopper on the "front" track.

The motor's worm-gear arrangement turns a sprocket and drives the bucket chain. One solenoid lifts the bin into position, the other opens the chute gate.

According to Lionel's service manual, the only material to be used with no. 97 is authentic no. 206 artificial coal. I don't know about that, but I *do* know a guy who uses kiln-dried Grape-Nuts with success.

Lubrication

There are plenty of theories floating around concerning the "right" lubricant. As far as I'm concerned, there are only two kinds: oil and grease. The important thing is that you use some-thing instead of nothing. The brand choice is up to you.

Lubricate the motor shaft at both end bearings. I use oil for this phase of lubrication, particularly if the motor has been idle for years or if it chatters during operation. Sometimes I'll follow with a dab of grease after the motor begins operating smoothly.

Next, oil the gear shaft bearings. Follow with a dab of grease, if you prefer. Coat all gears with grease. If the solenoid plungers stick, spray their shafts with TV tuner cleaner and work them by hand until they are free. It's best to avoid lubricating the chute gate unless it's absolutely necessary and then *only* from the bottom. Refer to fig. 1 for all the important lubrication points on your no. 97.

Cleaning

All external surfaces on your no. 97 should be cleaned—that's a given. Use a mild dishwashing detergent diluted with water on a clean rag and wipe everything down. Do this cleaning periodically, especially the chain and bucket assembly.

Clean no. 97's motor the same way you would a locomotive's motor. See Project 1. The most important parts are the commutator face, brushes, and brush wells. Each must be free of dirt and

Fig. 3. The lift mechanism's pucks ensure a centered and properly tensioned chain assembly. Make sure they move freely during no. 97's operation.

There is no formal adjustment process for no. 97—that means it's a free-lanced affair. If the bin's solenoid is binding, loosen the screw shown in fig. 2 and move the entire elevator structure left or right until the bind is eliminated. You may only minimize the binding, but that's okay. Tighten the screw after you've finished.

Make sure the two spring-loaded rubber pucks illustrated in fig. 3 move freely on their shaft. The pucks act as centering devices for the chain during operation. They also maintain the proper tension on the chain when things are moving.

And since all wiring is exposed, repairing or replacing any segment is simple. Use 20- or 22-gauge stranded wire and solder all connections. Check fig. 1 for wiring paths. If the motor or solenoids burn out, they'll have to be rewound professionally. In fact, you're better off searching swap meets or contacting parts dealers who advertise in *Classic Toy Trains*.

grease to provide optimum performance. Spray TV tuner cleaner (available from Radio Shack) directly on the commutator face's slots. In extreme cases, you may need to disassemble the motor for a thorough cleaning. Relubricate everything after reassembling.

The 164 log loader makes a great addition to any layout or collection. Its steady though noisy operation always draws plenty of attention.

PROJECT 18

Lumber Loader No. 164

Introduced in the 1940 consumer catalog, Lionel's no. 164 log loader was among the few prewar accessories also marketed after the war.

Lionel's no. 164 lumber loader is one of a handful of accessories that has all the charm and color of its prewar heritage. Its continued sales success resulted in its being cataloged with the newer and less expensive no. 364 log loader for three years. The no. 1654 first appeared in the 1940 catalog and was known as a "lumber loader," "lumber shed," and "chain-drive log loader." Even though it was a lot less messy than the no. 97 coal elevator, introduced two years before, the log loader was as much fun to operate.

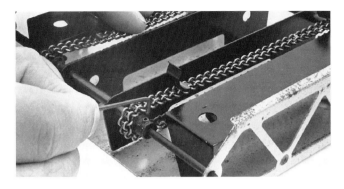 

Fig. 1. The Allen screws hold the sprockets tightly in place and maintain proper alignment of the chain hooks.

Fig. 2. For the release mechanism to operate properly, all the rods must be straight, pivots and linkages tight, and cranks vertical.

General Maintenance

If your log loader doesn't work, begin by checking the wiring. Look for damaged insulation, broken wires, and bad solder connections. The most common problem is with the three-conductor cable leading to the controller: The insulation tends to dry out and break away. Replacement cable is available from parts dealers. If the controller is missing, build a replacement with a single-pole single-throw toggle switch and a push button. See Project 6.

Often the lights don't work, even though the bulbs test fine. This is because power is transmitted through a metal rod that's subject to severe oxidation. Remove the rod, then sand the contact surfaces until the oxidation is gone.

The no. 164 is powered by a small, one-directional motor that revs fast and requires basic cleaning often. Since the motor is held in place by one screw, it can be dropped down for easier service. See Project 1.

Both ends of the armature shaft must be kept oiled. Oil all of the shaft bearings and grease the worm gears.

Lubricating chains and sprockets is a matter of personal preference. A light film of grease on the underside of the chain links may provide smoother operation for a while. However, grease attracts dust, and soon you have a black, gunky mess on the chains, hooks, and logs. Don't grease the chain unless you plan to clean it often.

As fig. 1 shows, the sprockets are held in place on the drive shaft with Allen set screws. If these become loose, the chain belts won't pull in tandem, the hooks will skew, and the logs will slide off before reaching the top. If this happens, align the hooks and tighten the set screws. There's no tension adjustment for the chain belts, but this rarely poses a problem.

One or more of the sheet-metal hooks may be missing, and finding replacements can be difficult. If you're handy, you can fashion your own hooks from sheet stock using an existing hook for a pattern. Or you can space out the hooks you have.

Release Mechanism

The unloading release mechanism is the part of the accessory most prone to trouble.

All the rods must be straight, pivots and linkages tight, and cranks perfectly vertical for the mechanism to work well (fig. 2). The stakes must be straight, tightly crimped to their activating shaft, and free from rubbing or binding in any position.

The most common problem is with the sheet-metal fasteners that hold the activating shaft between the stakes. They should be tight enough to hold the shaft in position without interference.

To get the release mechanism to function freely, remove the protective cover and move the solenoid plunger by hand, making adjustments as you go along.

Fortunately, this release mechanism assembly is the same as the one used on the 3651 and 3811 operating log cars. If you need replacement parts, you can scavenge them from one of these prewar cars. The loader used stakes from the 3811 car (3651 stakes are shorter, but will work).

Ready to Roll

The no. 164 log loader operates best at between 12 and 14 volts. I recommend wiring it directly to the appropriate fixed-voltage terminals on the transformer.

PLUMMER'S HELPER

Name and Number: Lumber loader no. 164

General maintenance: Keep motor tuned, cleaned, and lubricated. Wipe dust and grime from exposed surfaces, particularly around moving parts.

Maintenance schedule: As necessary.

Troubleshooting:

1. Motor malfunctions—Motor needs tune-up.

2. Electrical—Most electrical circuit problems are due to faulty three-conductor cable to controller. Check for short circuits, broken wires, and improper hook-up.

3. Faulty release mechanism—Check that solenoid function throws without binding. Straighten and tighten rods, pivots, linkages, and cranks to optimize thrust. Normal wear can loosen these. Recrimp stakes, if needed.

4. Loose chains—Align visually and tighten sprocket set screws.

5. Intermittent lighting. Sand oxidized contacts on metal roof rod.

6. Lamp replacement—Bulb no. 430 (27-3)

PROJECT 19

Automatic Gateman Nos. 45 and 145

Lionel's nos. 145 (left) and 45 (right) automatic gatemen are easy to find as they are among the most popular accessories Lionel made and were cataloged for many years.

There's a bright headlight coming 'round the bend. The smartly uniformed gateman throws open the shanty door, red lantern in hand, and halts oncoming automobile traffic just in time for the train to speed past. Then without any fanfare, he returns to his shanty to wait patiently for the next train charging through Lionelville.

Introduced in Standard and O gauge versions in 1935, the Lionel automatic gateman was destined to become the most popular toy train accessory in the world. It remained in continuous production until 1984. But his retirement didn't last long. Three years later, by popular demand, the gateman reappeared.

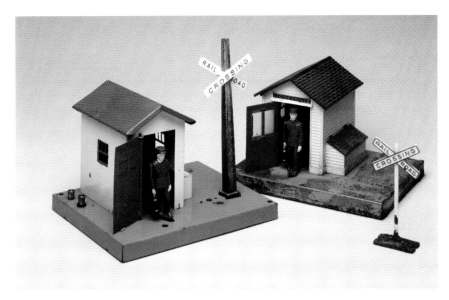

A little time and some paint from a local hardware store will make these men in blue proud to once again be of service to motorists and railroad alike.

Numbers 45, 045, and 45N, produced between 1935 and 1949, had a sheet-metal shanty. Starting in 1950, the gateman was housed in a plastic shanty (nos. 145, 2145, and 12713). For purposes of this article, gatemen cataloged through 1949 are referred to as Type A. Those cataloged in the years since are referred to as Type B.

Basic Operation

Although our man in blue is quite reliable, old age sometimes slows down his trip from shanty to trackside. But with attentive care and some basic repair and refinishing, he can look as good and function as well as he did during his youth.

The mechanical action of the gateman is identical no matter which version you have. As the train approaches, the door opens and the gateman comes out, swinging his lantern. Type A has a red light that shines when the door opens, simulating the lantern's glow. Type B features continuous lighting inside the shanty.

A single solenoid with a return spring moves the door and the gateman on both types. The complex linkage of cranks and levers devised for Type A (fig. 1) gave way to more reliable rack-and-pinion gearing on Type B models (fig. 2).

The accessory is hooked up to either a no. 145-C or 153-C contactor or an insulated section of track (fig. 3). Since the automatic gateman is designed to be operated on 12 to 14 fixed volts, this is the minimum recommended for snappy action and steady illumination.

However, there are times when track power is preferable. For instance, if the automatic gateman is located on a yard track where trains sometimes remain stationary, fixed voltage keeps the solenoid energized even if power to the locomotive is shut off. In this situation, constant voltage to the accessory could cause the coil to overheat and eventually lead to warpage or burnout.

Routine Maintenance

As old operating accessories go, both the prewar and postwar versions of the Lionel gatemen are amazingly durable. Provided they haven't been abused or improperly stored, they'll usually function without much bother. As a general rule, if it works, don't try to fix it. The leading problem, sluggish performance, is often the result of years of inactivity. Before you start a major surgical procedure, try to resuscitate the gateman with

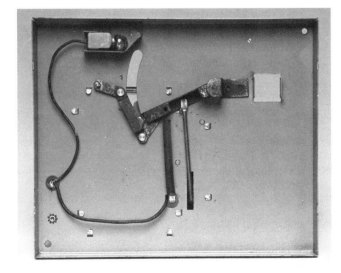

Fig. 1. The no. 45 automatic gateman used this system of cranks and levers.

Fig. 2. The no. 145 included this rack-and-pinion gearing arrangement.

about 25 cathartic jolts of 14 volts. Usually that's all that's needed to free up the action.

Bulb replacement is another routine procedure. Most Type A units have a socket mounted in a hinged fixture. Swing this out to gain access to the bulb. Change the bulb in a Type B by removing the shanty roof and bending the spring-steel socket arm upward.

If the figure has worked itself loose from the hexagonal mounting stud, use a drop or two of super glue to lock the feet in position. If the right arm is missing, you'll need to replace it.

Because there were so many shade variations in Lionel's blue plastic over the decades, the biggest problem with an arm transplant is finding one that matches the rest of the body. Once you do locate one, secure the new arm with a small dot of glue. Avoid getting the glue on the arm itself. If you can't find an exact match, but mismatched blue bothers you, either replace the entire figure or make up a story about how the gateman buys his jackets wholesale!

Any further treatment requires removing the sheet-metal bottom stamping, which is held in place by four tabs. These tabs tend to break off easily. Use a pair of small needlenose pliers to bend them carefully, just far enough to free the bottom. Even if you do, you'll be lucky to keep three of the tabs intact when you put everything back together. For that reason, ol' Ray recommends that all maintenance, troubleshooting, and refinishing be done at the same time.

That Healthy Glow

Both accessories in the opening photo of this article needed to be completely refinished, including new paint. Although a repaint may sound frightening at first, the project is easy since no masking is required and all the colors are available in ordinary aerosol spray-paint cans.

Before I worked on the appearance of the accessories, I

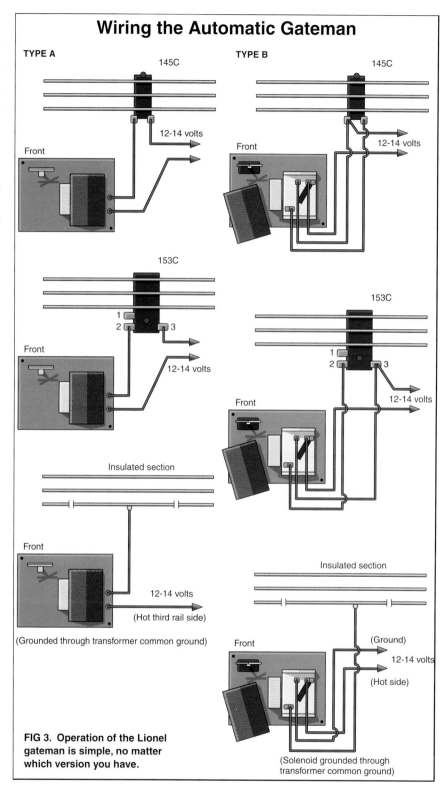

Wiring the Automatic Gateman

FIG 3. Operation of the Lionel gateman is simple, no matter which version you have.

made sure the mechanisms functioned properly. The accompanying Plummer's Helper includes a list of common ailments and simple cures.

Once you're ready to paint, start by disassembling the entire accessory (fig. 4). Use semi-paste

paint remover to strip the paint from all the metal parts except the base assembly of the 45N. Don't remove the solenoid and mechanical linkages from the bottom of the baseplates. Instead, cover them with masking tape. Since you can't use paint remover in

Name and Number: Operating gateman nos. 45 and 145
General maintenance: Little usually required. Keep the accessory clean. Replace burned-out bulb.
Maintenance schedule: As needed.
Troubleshooting:
1. Accessory dead—Check for loose or broken wires, burned-out solenoid.
2. Accessory buzzes but doesn't function—Check for distorted solenoid, frozen plunger, or locked-up linkage. Replace distorted solenoid. Clean plunger. Lubricate linkage; start with WD-40.
3. Sluggish action—Increase power to as high as 18 volts, if necessary. Clean plunger. Lubricate linkages. Apply thin layer of grease to underside of base near semicircular slot. Return spring may be weak—replace it.
4. Door doesn't close completely—Shorten or replace return spring. Check for bent hinge pin. Rack may have jumped a pinion gear cog.
5. Gateman rubs against base—Insert spacer washer under him.
6. Gateman loose—Use super glue.
7. Door rubs against base—Bend door hinges slightly, or carefully file a little off the bottom of the door.
8. Bulb—Lionel used a number of different bulbs over the years. The earlier units used small-globe red ones. Later units had standard 14-volt no. 363. I suggest using an 18-volt bulb. It gives realistic illumination, but is less likely to shine through the plastic shanty walls.

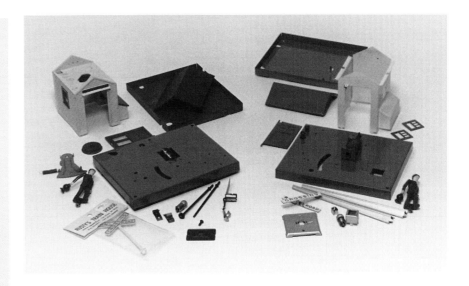

Fig. 4. One of Lionel's most popular accessories broken down into basic components. Be particularly careful when removing the tabs on the base.

those areas, grind the paint away with a stiff-bristled wire wheel. Attack any stubborn patches of rust with a wire wheel and a Scotchbrite pad.

Next, wash the components in warm, soapy water and set them aside to dry. Rub all the surfaces that will be painted with a tack cloth (available at paint and hardware stores) to remove any dust or dirt that can affect the paint finish.

Now you're ready to paint. Follow the paint manufacturer's directions, wear proper hand and eye protection, and spray in a well-ventilated area. It's better to use several light coats than try to cover everything with one heavy coat. Although it takes more time to spray multiple coats, the added time shows in the results.

Give the base at least four light coats of Ace Hardware Empire Green enamel spray paint. Red parts, such as the roof, windows, and door, require the same number of applications of Ace Hardware Banner Red. Give the shanty five coats of Krylon Antique White. Paint the crossbuck post Krylon Dull Aluminum. In my case, the die-cast crossbuck didn't need to be repainted, though I did enhance the lettering with a black marker.

The plastic roof and crossbuck on the no. 145 were a challenge because a previous owner had slopped some brown paint on them in an attempt at weathering. Since paint strippers can't be used on plastic without disastrous results, I soaked the pieces in a strong solution of laundry detergent and water for two weeks. While I've had luck using this method to remove unwanted paint in the past, it didn't work this time, and the brown paint remained.

I replaced the crossbuck with a reproduction piece and painted the roof with Testor's Dark Red, which is a close match and won't attack plastic as most regular spray enamels do. When the red had dried, I gave the roof a light dusting of Testor's Dullcote to hide the shine. After that had dried completely, I reassembled the two gateman. Both refinished accessories (fig. 5) were put aside until I found the time to install them on the layout.

By following these simple guidelines for maintenance and repair, you'll ensure that Lionel's seasoned little veteran will be spry and dapper and still manning his post well into the 21st century.

PROJECT 20

Searchlight Cars Nos. 3520 and 3620

No. 3620 SEARCHLIGHT CAR $7.95
Finely detailed well-car carries GM-type generator and big light which rotates continuously. It does not require a remote control track section, as it picks up current from the tracks. Measures 10" long.

Repairing Lionel's postwar searchlight cars, like this no. 3520, is an easy task using the author's tips.

I f the postwar Lionel searchlight cars had been real railroad cars, I'm not sure what their function would have been. Perhaps they would have scanned the sky above the tracks for enemy bombers, announced a grand opening or movie premiere, or disturbed the slumber of people living in houses adjacent to the right-of-way.

Whatever their function, watching an automatically rotating searchlight beacon going by on a freight or work train was a major nocturnal pastime in the Lionelville of the 1950s. At least, if the beacons were working correctly.

Several problems with the rotating beacon can crop up on cars collectors find today. Fortunately, it's simple to rectify them and get them working again.

How They Worked

The searchlight housing on the 3520 and 3620 cars rotates because it's part of a simple Lionel vibration motor (or "vibrotor"). Alternating current passing through an electric driving coil causes the stamped-steel bottom of the searchlight housing to vibrate at 60 cycles per second.

A rubber driving washer, with little "fingers" molded into it and positioned between the coil and the housing, advances the rotation of the searchlight in small increments 60 times a second. The effect is one of continuous rotation.

Lionel cemented the rubber driving washer to the inside of the searchlight housing on all but the earliest models. The cars from the first production runs have the washer cemented to their driving coil spools. Where the washer was placed makes no difference; the direction of rotation is the same.

The sequential on-off switch mechanism controls both the bulb and the driving coil. It may be operated by the electromagnet in a UCS or no. 6019 track by pressing the "uncouple" button when the car is centered over the track. Or it can be moved by hand by pulling down and releasing the trigger plate.

A ratchet-and-pawl device advances the contact drum to either an on or off position. Because the parts are riveted in place and the entire mechanism is covered by a plastic generator housing, the switch is rarely a source of major trouble unless it's been abused in some way.

Common Problems

Worn or broken fingers on the driving washer are the most common cause of faulty searchlight rotation. Replacements are available from most Lionel parts dealers. Some have adhesive backings, some don't. Lionel originally used a double-sided adhesive washer between the driving washer and the housing.

The fiber board upon which the switch mechanism is built is attached to the underside of the car with a speed nut. If loose, the speed nut can usually be tightened by gently tapping it with a punch and a small hammer.

A flickering light and/or an erratically operating motor are usually caused by dirt on the third-rail pickup roller or the switch contacts or both. Clean these by spraying the roller or switch contacts with TV tuner cleaner. They also can be swabbed with mineral spirits or alcohol. *Remember to use any of these flammable liquids carefully in a well-ventilated area.*

Sometimes the return spring on the switch mechanism can break or pop out of place. The trigger plate then loses its return function and will not operate reliably. If the spring is out of place, return its end to its mooring hole and apply a few drops of epoxy cement to keep it there. If the spring is broken, replacement springs are available from Lionel parts dealers.

Let There Be Light

After several hours running this car around your layout, you also may find that the light simply burns out. I usually replace them with a no. 1445, 18-volt, 0.15-amp bulb. It's not as bright as the original bulb, but it's not as hot either.

With a little finesse, you'll find that your nos. 3520 and 3620 searchlight cars are back up to speed and lighting up the night skies again over Lionelville.

A Lionel vibration motor (or "vibrotor") used alternating current to vibrate the housing.

The driving washer may have worn or broken fingers that keep the light from rotating. Replacement washers are available from most Lionel parts dealers. Lionel originally employed a double-sided adhesive washer.

Freight Station No. 356

Operating freight station no. 356 was introduced in 1952 and is a reliable, low-maintenance accessory—once you get it adjusted!

Lionel's no. 356 operating freight station and its modern era counterpart, no. 2324, can really please a crowd. It's easy to see why—a pair of demented baggage truck drivers chase each other around the platform at high speed on empty baggage carts! (Well, at least that's how it looks.)

An ingenious, if cumbersome, mechanism moves the carts. A metal plate suspended over the station platform vibrates vertically, bouncing the carts, which have rubber pads with directional "fingers" mounted on their undersides (fig. 1). This interaction between pad and platform causes the carts to move horizontally, which they do quite quickly if the input voltage is high.

Lionel provided two baggage trucks in contrasting colors. A latching mechanism in the station house itself holds one of the carts inside until the second truck enters the house, hitting the release trigger and allowing the first truck to leave (fig. 2). The action keeps going, and going, and going, for as long as you can stand the humming. Because of the orientation of the latch and trigger, the carts must go counterclockwise.

An electromagnetic coil, mounted in the center of the metal platform, causes the platform to vibrate when an AC voltage is

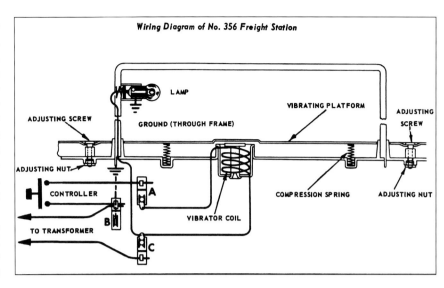

The no. 356 has a light as well as a vibrator coil.

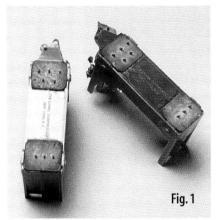

Fig. 1

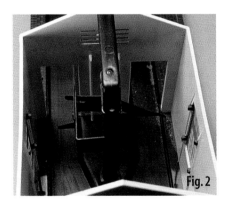

Fig. 2

Fig. 3

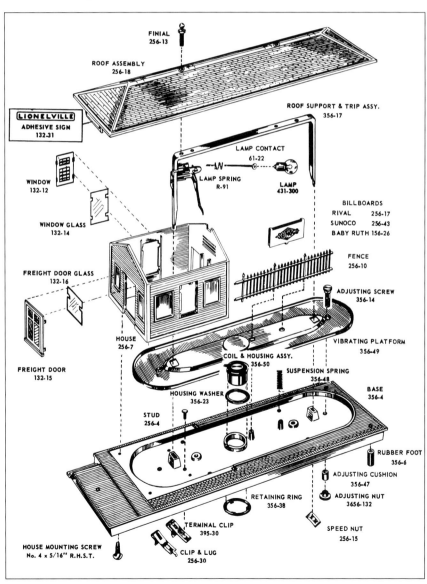

An exploded view of the no. 356.

applied. This apparatus is the famed Lionel "vibrotor" at its simplest. A no. 364C or other single-pole single-throw switch sends electricity to the vibrating coil.

The size of the air gap between the platform and the coil, along with the voltage applied, determines the intensity of the vibration. If you need to, you can widen or narrow the air gap using a pair of adjusting nuts that are located at the ends of the platform, under the station (fig. 3). When properly adjusted, the platform should have some freedom of motion but should not touch the base.

Either screwing in the roof finials too tightly or screwing the station to the layout too firmly can dampen the vibration and hinder proper operation. Leave the finials finger-tight, and leave a gap between any mounting screws and the platform. If you're installing your station permanently, be sure to drill large holes through the benchwork under the adjusting nuts before you install the station so that you can reach the nuts later.

Although virtually all the baggage trucks came from Lionel without loads, several vendors now offer loads for them. If you decide to add loads to your carts, load both; otherwise the carts will travel at different speeds.

Lionel recommended operating the station at between 12 and 14 volts AC. As with most vibrotor-powered accessories, though, it's even easier to fine-tune your station if you can power it via a variable-voltage tap on your transformer. That way you can adjust the intensity of the vibration without having to pick up your station or crawl under your layout. The lamp needs approximately 12 volts as well.

A no. 356 is a fun and nearly trouble-free accessory, and they're available at bargain prices (relatively speaking). Tune yours (or buy one) and put it into service on your layout today!

Name and Number: Operating freight station no. 356

General maintenance: Keep platform clean and in adjustment for maximum vibration.

Maintenance schedule: As needed.

Troubleshooting:

1. Accessory doesn't operate—Check for loose or broken wire, burned-out motor coil. Repair and/or replace as needed.

2. Sluggish operation—Adjust air gap between coil and platform with the two adjusting nuts until maximum "buzz" is heard at the fixed voltage. Or increase voltage slightly.

3. Carts pile up inside station—Check trigger and latch mechanism to see that it operates freely. Bend if necessary.

4. Carts travel at uneven or unequal speeds—Worn or broken "fingers" on the rubber pads under the carts. Replacements are available.

5. Bulb—Lionel used a 14-volt, bayonet-base 431-300. I prefer an 18-volt bulb—it gives lower, more realistic illumination.